P9-AGH-659

ACKNOWLEDGMENTS

A book covering the kinds of subjects found within these pages is often only as good as the information the author has drawn upon to write. Finding reliable sources of background and historical information often requires soliciting advice and information from a range of experts in various fields, and many people helped me in my research. I would like to take this opportunity to specifically thank some who were especially helpful.

Louis Campbell, curator of the Siuslaw Pioneer Museum, compiled a collection of stories and historical details on the ghost of Heceta House and gave valuable suggestions on where I could find additional information. Staff members at the Tillamook Pioneer Museum were extremely helpful in recommending sources for researching the lost beeswax galleon and the history of the Spanish treasure ships.

Finally, two people who have helped me with this and past book projects include Steve Lent, of the Bowman Museum, Crook County Historical Society, who brought me up to speed on the latest developments in the search for the lost Blue Bucket Mine and provided historical photographs; and Todd Shaffer, reference archivist with the Oregon State Archives and one of the best and most efficient photographic researchers I have ever worked with.

Finally, I also drew on a wide range of published reference material, including popular books and magazine articles, scholarly works, and news reports. To all who helped me with this project, directly and indirectly, I offer my sincere thanks. You will find them all credited in the bibliography section at the end of this book.

MYSTERIES AND LEGENDS

OF OREGON

MYSTERIES AND LEGENDS SERIES

MYSTERIES AND LEGENDS

OF OREGON

TRUE STORIES
OF THE UNSOLVED AND UNEXPLAINED

JIM YUSKAVITCH

Guilford, Connecticut

Copyright © 2010 Morris Book Publishing, LLC

Project editor: Jessica Haberman
Layout: Sue Murray
Text design: Lisa Reneson, Two Sisters Design
Map: Daniel Lloyd © Morris Book Publishing, LLC

Library of Congress Cataloging-in-Publication Data
Yuskavitch, James.
  Mysteries and legends of Oregon : true stories of the unsolved and
unexplained / Jim Yuskavitch.
      p. cm.
  Includes bibliographical references and index.
  ISBN 978-0-7627-5016-0
  1. Oregon—History—Anecdotes. 2. Oregon—Biography—Anecdotes. 3.
Curiosities and wonders—Oregon—Anecdotes. 4. Legends—Oregon. I.
Title.
  F876.6.Y86 2010
  398.209795—dc22
                                      2009029503
Printed in the United States of America
10 9 8 7 6 5 4 3 2 1

CONTENTS

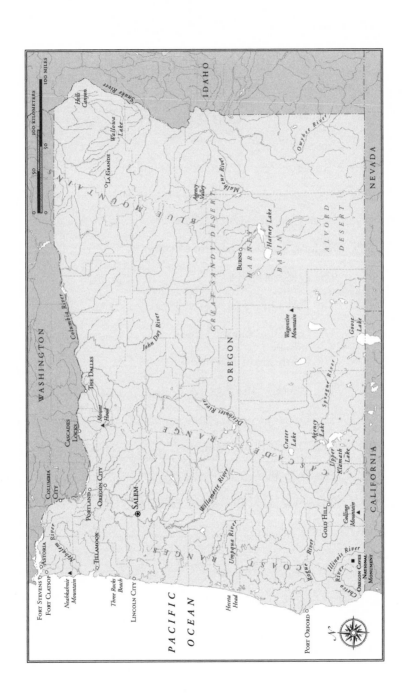

INTRODUCTION

Researching and writing *Mysteries and Legends of Oregon* was a wild and entertaining ride, indeed. The words *mysteries* and *legends* cover such a wide field of truth and reality. Are all legends fables, or are they informed by some (or much) truth? Are some mysteries better left unsolved? As I pored over tales from the oddball and dusty reaches of Oregon's past, I marveled at the range they encompassed, taking in age-old mythologies such as sea monsters and Native American legends along with subjects seemingly lifted from the pages of comic books, horror movie matinees, and frontier adventures and then mixed together into stories that in their own way tell us something about Oregon and the people who have populated the place over the centuries.

So, in a sense, the tales you will read here are an Oregon history of sorts, for no matter how unbelievable the recounting may seem or how outlandish the claims of those who appear in these stories, history is the theme that runs through them all.

The ratio of historical truth to fable and fiction varies, but all seek to explain events that have occurred, or were thought to have occurred, and things seen, or believed to have been seen. A few of these narratives are mostly true—historical mysteries still unsolved—and none of them are completely fictional.

These stories also reflect different parts of the state, their geographies, the hardships the people who lived in those areas faced, and the things they considered dark, mysterious, and fearful. Deep forest and deep water are two ubiquitous aspects of the Oregon landscape where human beings have often been wary to venture, and their unknowns manifest themselves as dangerous creatures that confound science and pose dire danger to all who encounter them. Hence, Bigfoot wanders the rain forests, and winged serpents slither in the roiling rivers and silent, remote lakes.

Explorers and pioneers played a major role in the early days of the Oregon Territory, and so, too, do they in the state's mysteries and legends. Pioneers disappear under mysterious circumstances, or set off in search of lost gold mines in the universal narrative that fortune, both good and bad, awaits wanderers in the wilderness. Many of the stories have roots in the oral traditions of Oregon's native peoples, roots from which the tales grew larger and blossomed over the decades.

Mysterious landscapes beget mysteries, and nowhere is this more true than on the coast, where the unknown sea has washed up many a riddle upon Oregon's beaches, related in stories of anonymous shipwrecks, sought but unfound buried treasure, and places where deceased occupants may still reside.

These are themes that run through this book and weave together into tales of an Oregon part known, part unknown, and part unknowable. I will leave it to you, the reader, to decide which is which.

CHAPTER 1

D. B. COOPER, MYSTERY HIJACKER

The eight-year-old boy, on a family outing on February 10, 1980, was wandering along the Columbia River near Portland, Oregon, when he spotted something partially buried in the sandy shoreline. Curiosity aroused, he began digging, soon revealing a pile of old, tattered, and water-spotted $20 bills, bundled together with rubber bands. There were 294 $20 bills in all, totaling $5,880. When Brian Ingram's family turned the cash over to authorities, the Federal Bureau of Investigation checked the bills' serial numbers against those known to have been involved in past crimes and criminal activities. What they discovered astounded them. The money was part of a $200,000 ransom paid to the skyjacker known only as D. B. Cooper nine years earlier. It was a saga that became a legend and began at the Portland airport, climaxing—but not ending—in the stormy night skies over the Pacific Northwest. It is the only unsolved airplane hijacking in U.S. history, and many decades later the search to discover the perpetrator's identity and fate remains unfinished.

D. B. Cooper FBI wanted poster

The legend of D. B. Cooper was born on November 24, 1971, the day before Thanksgiving, when a man later described as in his mid-forties, nearly six feet tall, with a dark complexion, wearing a dark raincoat, white shirt, a dark tie, and sunglasses, and carrying a briefcase bordered a Northwest Orient (now Northwest Airlines) Boeing 727 at the Portland airport bound for Seattle, Washington. The name on his ticket, for which he paid $18.52, was Dan Cooper.

Soon after the mid-afternoon takeoff, Cooper, occupying seat number 18C near the back of the plane, leaned forward and handed a note to flight attendant Florence Schaffner, who was strapped into a nearby jump seat. Thinking that the passenger had romantic designs and was giving her his phone number, she put it aside with barely a glance. But the mystery man in the dark sunglasses leaned over and suggested she read it now. Schaffner took the note back out and unfolded it. To her shock, it said that the man in seat 18C had a bomb in his briefcase and that he was hijacking Northwest Orient Flight 305. But there was more. The note demanded a ransom of $200,000, four parachutes—two main chutes and two emergency chutes—and instructions for how everything was to be carried out. Those instructions directed the crew to land at Seattle-Tacoma International Airport, where the parachutes and ransom money should be brought on board. Once that phase of the hijacking was completed, additional instructions would be forthcoming. Any funny business and Cooper would detonate the bomb in his suitcase. Then the hijacker gave Schaffner a peek just to let her know that he meant business. Inside the briefcase she saw bright red cylinders, a battery, and a tangle of wires that looked like it could very well have been an explosive device.

Schaffner hurried off to the flight deck to tell Captain William Scott, First Officer William Rataczak, and Second Officer Harold E. Anderson about this unexpected development while another flight attendant, Tina Mucklow, sat down next to Cooper to keep an eye on him.

With the instructions relayed and a course set for Seattle, Captain Scott radioed his bosses at Northwest Orient to apprise them of the situation. Ordered to cooperate completely with Cooper, authorities on the ground, and the FBI in particular, scrambled to meet his demands and come up with a plan to foil him. Cooper enjoyed his flight to Seattle chatting, reportedly politely and amicably, with the flight attendants, drinking whiskey, and smoking Raleigh cigarettes. When the jet landed at Seattle-Tacoma at about 5:40 p.m. with its six-member crew, thirty-six passengers, and one hijacker, the money and the parachutes were waiting.

In his instructions, Cooper had specifically asked for unmarked bills, and FBI agents feared that if they marked the cash anyway and were discovered, he might detonate the bomb. So they honored his request. But they had a trick up their sleeve. FBI agents used $20 bills that were printed in 1969, since their serial numbers mainly began with an *L*. Then they created a microfilm record of all ten thousand bills so that each serial number would be on file. Because Cooper's ransom note didn't specify denominations for the money, the FBI chose $20 bills to make his load bulkier and more difficult to manage.

Cooper had also requested sport parachutes rather than military parachutes, which authorities eventually found on short notice at a skydiving school in Issaquah, Washington.

Rolling to a stop on an out-of–the-way tarmac for refueling and further instructions with the cabin lights turned down to foil police snipers, Cooper examined the cash, which was in a white laundry bag, and the parachutes that had been delivered to the plane by courier. Satisfied that everything was in order, he released all thirty-six passengers and two of the flight attendants, keeping Scott, Rataczak, Anderson, and flight attendant Mucklow on board for the next leg of the hijacking, a trip to Mexico City.

Cooper also had some specific instructions on how the plane was to get there, including flying with the wing flaps down at 15 degrees, an airspeed of less than 200 miles per hour, at an altitude of less than 10,000 feet, and with the aircraft's rear door open and the stairway lowered. He also demanded that the aircraft's cabin be depressurized, presumably to reduce the suction created when the stairway door was opened in preparation for his aerial escape. The crew explained that by flying with that configuration, excess drag would be created and they would burn too much fuel to make it nonstop to Mexico City. The plane would have to land in Reno, Nevada, to refuel if they were to have any chance of reaching their final destination. After some convincing, Cooper agreed to the change in plans. By 8:00 p.m. the 727 was back in the air heading south, following the western slope of the Cascade Mountains and directly into stormy, rainy weather. Unbeknownst to Cooper, several U.S. Air Force F-106 jet fighters had been dispatched from the 318th Fighter Interceptor Squadron stationed at McChord Air Force Base, Washington, to shadow the jetliner and hopefully mark the location when and if he parachuted from the plane.

Once airborne, pilot Scott lowered the plane's rear staircase. At that point Cooper ordered Tina Mucklow, who was in the seat next to him for takeoff, to go forward and close the curtain that separated the first-class and coach compartments, and he warned her not to come back. This was the last time anyone saw Cooper, and accounts on exactly what happened next vary. But a reasonably accurate picture of what transpired over the ensuing tense minutes can be painted.

Cooper retreated to the back of the plane, where the deployed staircase yawned into the black sky. By now, the aircraft was over southwestern Washington and was rapidly approaching the Columbia River and the Oregon border. A heavy storm, with high winds and pelting rain, raged outside. To make conditions even worse for someone contemplating a skydive, a low cover of clouds prevented any light from the ground from penetrating into the sky. This situation made any visual orientation virtually impossible.

With the wind howling in the blackness out the rear door, Cooper somehow strapped the bag of cash to his body and then donned a main chute and an emergency chest chute, picking them from the four that the FBI had provided. Around 8:20 p.m. or so, the jet's crew felt a "bump" that could have been made by someone climbing out onto the rear stairs and jumping, but no one saw such an event—even the jet fighter pilots tailing the airliner, whose visibility was severely limited by the stormy weather.

Some reports say the crew tried to contact Cooper via intercom when he retreated aft, to which he either curtly responded or did not respond at all. Other reports say there was no effort to further communicate with him until the plane touched down in Reno around 8:30 p.m. But by then Cooper was gone.

Once the plane was on the tarmac at Reno, Captain Scott did try to make contact with Cooper by intercom. Receiving no reply, he walked to the back of the plane and found it empty. Meanwhile, FBI agents and local police officers surrounded the airport and the plane. When Scott confirmed to authorities that Cooper was gone, they came on board to conduct an investigation, interview witnesses, and collect evidence.

Among the first things investigators discovered were the two chutes Cooper had left behind. That blew their theory that the hijacker had requested two sets of parachutes because he had an accomplice on board. The other thing they noticed was that the emergency chest chute Cooper had chosen to strap on was one that had been used by the skydiving school for classroom demonstrations and would not open. That error was inadvertent on the part of the FBI and the skydiving school, which supplied the demo chute accidentally in the rush to meet the sky pirate's demands. Cooper had jumped with a nonfunctioning emergency parachute.

Next came a sweep of the cabin for evidence, eyewitness accounts of the crime, and obtaining a description of the suspect. In the back of the plane, along with the two parachutes, investigators found Cooper's tie and a mother-of-pearl tie clip. They dusted for fingerprints and collected several dozen, although none of them were necessarily those of the suspect. Interviews with witnesses also allowed the FBI to create a composite sketch of Cooper for use on wanted posters.

Now the manhunt would begin in earnest. Based on where the crew of Flight 305 felt the "bump," investigators, consulting with skydiving experts, identified an area of about twenty-eight square miles in southwestern Washington where Cooper might have touched down. FBI agents and local sheriff's deputies conducted the ground search by foot and helicopter. Months passed, and by the end of winter all attempts to find Cooper—or some evidence of his landing, whether it be his parachute hanging in a tree or his remains—had turned up empty-handed.

In March 1972, a more intense search was conducted, and at least two hundred U.S. Army personnel from Fort Lewis participated. The search, which remains the most intensive manhunt ever launched in the Pacific Northwest, lasted for six weeks. In the end, they found nothing, and the search was called off. However, it wasn't the end of the hijacking saga, but just the beginning.

Ironically, the most prominent piece of the legend—the name D. B. Cooper, by which the hijacker is most widely known—was the result of a communications mix-up. When word got out that a hijacking was in progress that November night, Portland-based FBI agent Ralph Himmelsbach immediately launched a search of the Portland Police Bureau's criminal records for any Dan Coopers, the name on the hijacker's plane ticket. There were none. But there was a D. B. Cooper, who had an arrest record on a series of disorderly conduct charges.

The word went out to law enforcement personnel to ascertain his whereabouts. Oregon State Police officers found him—at home watching television as the hijacking was unfolding, eliminating him as a suspect. But when newspaper reporters had called the police earlier in the day, the clerk on duty told them they were searching for a suspect named D. B. Cooper. After he was cleared, a correction went out to the press. But the name D. B. Cooper had stuck in the public imagination, and the hijacker has been called that ever since. The television-watching D. B. Cooper would be the first of what would eventually become more than a thousand suspects, all of whom so far have led to dead ends.

In November 1976, even though he had not been captured, U.S. Assistant Attorney Jack Collins in Portland sought an indictment against D. B. Cooper as a "John Doe" for air piracy. The FBI expanded its efforts by circulating the list of serial numbers of the ransom money throughout the world, and Northwest Airlines offered a reward of up to $25,000 to anyone who could recover all or even a portion of the stolen money. But there were no takers, and slowly the trail of D. B. Cooper went cold.

Even as the active investigation began to ebb, the essential question was whether Cooper had successfully parachuted into the mountains and then made his way to safety with the loot in hand, or whether he had died during the jump. Initial theories pegged him as an expert skydiver with military training, perhaps a paratrooper, who confidently and carefully planned a difficult jump from a commercial aircraft to a predesignated location where an accomplice on the ground helped him escape. That theory began to fall apart as investigators looked more deeply. The idea of Cooper as an expert paratrooper went down first, largely based on the fact that an experienced skydiver would have recognized that jumping from a jetliner in a ferocious storm was extremely risky and probably would not have gone through with it. Second, given the turbulent conditions that night, there was no way that he could have arranged to meet a partner at a specific landing site. Even a slight change in the wind could cause a parachutist to drift many miles from his intended destination. The odds that a helper was waiting for Cooper on the ground were slim to none. In fact, the FBI believed that, even though no body or other proof had been located, he did not survive the jump and was almost certainly dead. It was even possible that between the shrieking storm, heavy rain, and lack of visible contact with the ground to orient himself, Cooper may have panicked and never even opened his chute, tumbling instead hundreds of miles per hour into the ground.

Nevertheless, because the case was still officially active, the FBI was bound to continue its investigation on the chance that a real lead would arise, and in the intervening years many suspects turned up.

The first lead came on April 7, 1972, while the active on-the-ground search for Cooper was still in progress. A man hijacked a United Airlines Boeing 727 during a stopover in Denver. The hijacker used nearly the same M.O. as Cooper. He handed a flight attendant a hijack note that instructed the plane to land in San Francisco, there to be provided with four parachutes and $500,000. Instead of a bomb in a briefcase, he was armed with an unloaded pistol and a paperweight hand grenade. Later that day, he used the rear stairs of the plane to bail out over Utah after the hijacked plane had departed San Francisco. But he made some mistakes, leaving his handwritten note on the plane and fingerprints on a magazine he was reading during the flight. Within two days, that evidence led the FBI to Richard McCoy Jr. of Provo, Utah. FBI agents found most of the cash hidden in his house. Arrested for the hijacking and convicted, he was sentenced to forty-five years in prison. But he, along with a number of other convicts, escaped in August 1974 and shortly thereafter was killed in a shootout with the law.

Although justice had been served in that instance, what was on everybody's mind was whether McCoy—an experienced skydiver—and D. B. Cooper were one and the same. But an investigation found that he was having dinner with his family on Thanksgiving 1971, the day of the Cooper heist. His alibi for that crime was ironclad, and, alas, he was just a copycat hijacker. The search for the real D. B. Cooper would go on.

The next trace of Cooper did not appear until four years later when a hunter found a placard containing instructions on how to operate the rear door and staircase of a Boeing 727 in the forest in southwest Washington. It was verified to have come from Northwest Flight 305.

The next lead was Brian Ingram's discovery of part of the ransom on the banks of the Columbia River. That discovery seemed to confirm investigators' long-held assessment that Cooper had died from his jump, as they felt the money the boy found had slowly washed down from the mountains over the years, probably originating somewhere in the forest where Cooper's bones now lay. Ingram was eventually allowed to keep $2,760 of the $5,880 he found. In 2008 he auctioned fifteen of the bills for $37,000. The rest of the money went to the airline's insurance company, with the FBI retaining fourteen bills for evidence.

In the intervening years, other suspects arose, some more prominent than others, and all eventually turned out to be false leads.

In 2000 Jo Weber of Pace, Florida, suspected that her late husband Duane L. Weber was D. B. Cooper, based on stories he told and innuendos he made to that effect. The FBI compared his fingerprints to those found on the hijacked plane, but no matches were found. In 2007 the FBI compared DNA taken from Cooper's tie, ruling out Weber as Cooper once and for all.

Another prime suspect surfaced in 2007. A man named Kenneth Christiansen was identified as a possible suspect in a *New York Times Magazine* article, published in October of that year. Christiansen, who had died in 1994, was a Northwest Airlines flight attendant, a resident of Washington state, and a former paratrooper who smoked heavily; according to his brother Lyle, who brought forward the theory, these characteristics made him a prime D. B. Cooper candidate (although some years earlier the FBI had determined that the hijacker was not a heavy smoker as is often assumed). The FBI soon dismissed Christiansen as a viable suspect largely because his physical description did not match Cooper's. In addition, as an experienced paratrooper, investigators doubted that Christiansen would have been foolish enough to jump in the weather conditions on the night of the hijacking.

The year 2008 turned out to be a big one for D. B. Cooper fans. In January the FBI announced that it was beginning a new effort to solve the case and identify the hijacker, and it made additional evidence available to the public on its Web site, hoping that someone may know something that will crack the case. Then, in March, several children in southwest Washington found an old parachute along a dirt road, raising a great deal of excitement that it might be Cooper's. Law enforcement officials took it to Earl Cossey, the man from the skydiving school who supplied the FBI with the four parachutes on the night of the hijacking. After examining it, he determined that it was not one of his chutes but was an older model, probably made in the mid-1940s.

Then, during the summer of 2008, U.S. and Canadian news outlets reported that a Spokane, Washington, lawyer working on a book about the hijacking theorized that a man named William Gossett was D. B. Cooper. Gossett, a former college teacher in Ogden, Utah, had retired to Depoe Bay on the Oregon coast and died there in September 2003, leaving, so it was said, much of the ransom money in a safe deposit box in a bank in Vancouver, British Columbia. He purportedly showed his son the keys to the safe deposit box and told him he was the real hijacker. The FBI has no solid evidence linking Gossett to the D. B. Cooper case.

In the world of criminal investigations, cold cases can sometimes heat up when least expected, and FBI agents are hoping that someday the same will happen to this high-profile, unsolved airline hijacking. Perhaps someday, somewhere, someone will remember something, a small detail that seemed unimportant at the time, or come across something suspicious. Maybe someone who knows more than they want to tell will slip up after a drink too many and talk, and someone else will pick up the phone and call the FBI. In the world of criminal investigations, a small thing can sometimes result in a big break. But until that break comes, no one knows whether D. B. Cooper reached solid earth safely that wet, wintry November night in 1971 and made off with the loot to live the high life, or whether he is somewhere in the mountains of the Pacific Northwest, a silent pile of bones, surrounded by decaying $20 bills and an old, tattered parachute as his shroud.

CHAPTER 2

BIGFOOT, THE WILD MAN OF OREGON

A hundred yards or so off the Collings Mountain Trail in the Siskiyou National Forest, not far from the California border, sits a large boxlike structure amid a grove of coniferous trees. It is about ten feet square at its base and more than eight feet high and has a welded steel gate that blocks its entrance-way. This odd structure is a trap that was designed to capture a Bigfoot, the legendary apelike beast that many believe roams the deep and remote forests of the Pacific Northwest from northern California to British Columbia. Since the early 1800s human wanderers of this far-flung region have reported, and continue to report, Bigfoot sightings and signs. And Oregon has long been regarded as a stronghold for these shy, mysterious, and fearsome creatures.

A now-dissolved Eugene, Oregon–based group called the North American Wildlife Research Team, which hoped to prove the forest apes' existence by capturing one, built the Bigfoot trap in 1974. For six years the organization's members baited the trap with animal carcasses and checked it regularly, but in the end all they ever caught were black bears. The world's only Bigfoot trap is now a tourist attraction that is maintained by the U.S. Forest Service, its door and latch mechanism disabled, never to capture its intended quarry. But true believers in the Bigfoot legend have far from abandoned the quest.

Bigfoot burst onto the national scene in 1958 when a road construction crew working in the Bluff Creek area in northern California discovered gigantic, eighteen-inch footprints—humanlike, but not quite. The news went out to the nation's newspapers over the wire services, accompanied by photographs of the man who discovered the tracks, Gerald Crew, holding a plaster cast made from one of the massive footprints.

In October 1967 another Bigfoot bombshell hit the news wires when Roger Patterson and Robert Gimlin filmed a large apelike animal walking in the Six Rivers National Forest in northern California, further riveting public interest in this strange, unknown beast.

Bigfoot is also known as Sasquatch, one of the names Native Americans called the beast in their own legends about this mythical creature. The natural history of Bigfoot is not well known but has been pieced together based on descriptions by people who claim to have seen one as well as assumptions about the habitat where they are believed to live. Eyewitnesses say that the creatures are stocky and large, from six to ten feet tall, weighing as much as eight hundred pounds, and cloaked in long hair that

*Oregon's deep, dark, mysterious rain forests are reputed to be
a favored haunt of Bigfoot.*

varies from dark brown to reddish. Bigfoot is generally presumed to be omnivorous and primarily nocturnal. The descriptions given of the animals by those who say they have encountered them are generally consistent and suggest that they are some kind of great ape. Although great apes are exclusively tropical animals, some people postulate that a Bigfoot's hairy body and large body mass help keep it warm in the Pacific Northwest's damp, cold, and snowy climate and that its less-than-picky diet, ranging from small animals to wild berries, allows it to make use of nearly every food source the forest has to offer.

While scientists remain universally skeptical of the beast's existence, some theories postulate what a Bigfoot might be if it is really out there. One theory claims that it is a new, undiscovered species of large primate that has so far been able to elude science. Another asserts that Bigfoot is a surviving population of *Gigantopithecus blacki,* an evolutionary precursor to the human race that lived in Asia and became extinct about 300,000 years ago. Advocates of this theory suggest that the species migrated over the Bering land bridge to establish itself in northwest North America, where it was somehow able to avoid the fate of annihilation that its Asian counterpart met.

The first recorded Bigfoot sign came in 1811 when Canadian trader and surveyor David Thompson claimed to have found a set of large footprints near the Athabasca River. At first he thought they were from a bear, but later he decided the prints came from some other unknown creature, perhaps a mysterious animal, a sasquatch, which local natives believed roamed the region. Since that first report, Bigfoot or its sign has been encountered on a regular basis throughout the Pacific Northwest. Over the decades, reports of Bigfoot in Oregon have been so numerous that it has prompted everything from the specially designed trap set in the Siskiyou National Forest to full-blown field expeditions intended to find one, record it on film, or perhaps even capture it.

Since the mid-1880s there have been more than six hundred reports of Bigfoot activity in Oregon, ranging from screams in the night to alleged glimpses of the animal as it fled into the forest. Clackamas County boasts the most Bigfoot activity by far with 122 reports, followed by Lane County with 57 and Deschutes with 37. Bigfoot has apparently never set foot in Malheur, Gilliam, Sherman, and Tillamook Counties, for no one has reported seeing one in those areas.

One of the first Oregon Bigfoot tales dates to 1885, when several hunters in Linn County claimed to have spotted a "hairy man" near Lebanon eating a deer in the forest, although no other details of the incident are available. In the late 1800s and early 1900s, loggers and prospectors lived, worked, and traveled in the wildest areas of Oregon in the heart of "Bigfoot country," so naturally some of the best Bigfoot yarns come from the mining and timber camps of that era. Some of the earliest and most action-packed encounters with the Oregon ape-men took place in Curry County in the remote, forested mountains of the southwestern part of the state.

In 1899 two men named Robbins and Benson, prospecting the Sixes River headwaters area in Curry County, were said to have spotted a six-and-a-half-foot-tall, yellowish, hairy animal they described as a "devil" throwing their camping gear off a cliff. The creature ran away when they took a few shots at it with their rifles. The next year some miners working the same area spied a nine-foot-tall "hairy man" drinking out of a small stream. Four years later Bigfoot again returned to the Sixes mining district, this time in a bad mood. The *Lane County Leader* newspaper reported that a "wild man" described as "Hairy, broad hands & feet and 7' tall" was spotted on three occasions near Myrtle Point. The wild man, perhaps taking umbrage at being shot at by some of the prospectors, "shook a cabin" and hurled rocks at one of its attackers.

One of the most dramatic and wildest Oregon Bigfoot stories is set in the late 1890s along the Chetco River in south-western Oregon. The story has it that a group of about a dozen loggers, their families in tow, had established a logging camp on the banks of the river, and each morning they headed out for a long day cutting down trees in the forest. But each morning they found the large, freshly cut logs they had carefully stacked the previous evening tumbled about the camp intermixed with strange, humanlike footprints, but much too large to be human. Perplexed, the men thought it must be the work of bears and vowed to shoot any that dared venture into their camp.

But late one night, horrible screams began emanating from the dense vegetation at the forest's edge. Grabbing a rifle and a torch, one brave fellow followed the sound into the dark forest. But before long, he returned, a look of sheer terror on his face as he described a monstrous beast, eight feet tall, covered with hair, with piercing yellow eyes and terrible fangs. The camp went into a panic as women and children headed for their tents and the men stood guard around the perimeter, a huge bonfire lighting up the night as an added measure of security, for all animals—even monsters—feared fire.

After an uneventful night and day, the men's nerves had calmed a little, and they concocted a plan to find and destroy this fearsome, unknown beast. That night, two volunteers stole quietly from camp armed with rifles and lanterns, determined to end this mysterious threat once and for all. As the men melted into the dark forest, the night's silence engulfed them—but not for long.

How long it took from the time they left camp to when their shrieks, shouts, and gunfire pierced the night's silence, as their companions back at camp listened in horror, has not been recorded. But it lasted only a few seconds. Then the woods fell silent once again. Determined to rescue their friends, several more loggers took up firearms and torches and went off in the direction from which that sickening cacophony came.

About a half mile from camp, they stumbled on a scene that caused them to stop and recoil in horror. What they beheld was a scene of total carnage, with the bodies of their two friends ripped to pieces. Entrails pasted against bark and blood dripping from branches and leaves provided graphic evidence that someone, or something, of incredible strength had swung the hapless loggers around like rag dolls, smashing them against trees and stumps until they were pulp. The huge, blood-filled footprints trailing off into the forest were the only sign of the murderous, hairy "wild man" of Oregon.

While all reports of Bigfoot encounters are unverifiable, most are not nearly as colorful and dramatic as the tale of the

Chetco River logging camp. They are more likely to involve foul smells and screams, said to be characteristic of Bigfoot, or a brief glance of a large, unidentified hairy creature in the shadows of the forest understory.

In the summer of 1953, a fisherman thought he spotted a Bigfoot watching him from the forest's edge along Alder Creek in Clackamas County. A large creature that continually whacked sticks as it went briefly followed a U.S. Forest Service geologist who was conducting trail reconnaissance work along the North Santiam River in 1967. Bigfoot's bloodlust again reared its head in the woods near Portland in 1977, when a young girl found her pet pony at the bottom of an embankment, its neck broken. She found long gray hairs that emanated a strange odor on the pony's carcass and a single set of seventeen-inch footprints nearby. In the fall of 1996, a husband and wife driving on U.S. Highway 97 south of La Pine in Deschutes County said they saw a "tall, rangy figure suddenly emerge from the cover of the treeline, about 150 feet ahead on [their] right, and stride determinedly toward the road across a grassy fringe."

Sometimes the encounters are more graphic, as was a night-time encounter with a Bigfoot by a retired police officer on a lonely road in the Umatilla National Forest in northeast Oregon. Driving his truck slowly up a steep grade on Highway 207, south of Hardman, at about 11:30 p.m. in late October 1980, he spotted out of the corner of his eye a large, hairy, upright creature standing on the fog line peering at him with glowing red eyes. The former lawman described the animal as about eight feet tall, with reddish hair that was about three or four inches long. Petrified at the sight and alone on a remote forest road where he was able to drive only 25 or 30 miles per hour on that incline and unable to speed past, all he could do was watch the creature as the creature watched him slowly go by. Afraid of being considered crazy, the retired officer waited years before coming forward to tell of his experience.

Not limited merely to the past, Oregon encounters with this legendary creature have continued, unabated, into the twenty-first century. A beast that has held on since the Pleistocene epoch is certainly not going to be deterred by a new millennium.

In fact, just seven months into the year 2000, a Bigfoot sighting occurred in Oregon Caves National Monument in Josephine County. On July 1 of that year, Matthew Johnson, his wife, and three children were hiking on the Big Tree Loop Trail when Johnson needed to make a short detour into the woods to relieve himself. Standing a bit off from the trail, he began to hear a strange noise he described as "whoa, whoa, whoa," accompanied by a disagreeable odor reminiscent of skunk. Noticing a brief motion in the forest, he turned to look, only to see Bigfoot staring back at him. Park rangers who interviewed him when he reported the encounter believe that the Grants Pass resident did indeed see something in the forest that day.

Since 2000 at least 140 suspected or claimed sightings of Bigfoot or Bigfoot sign have been reported in Oregon, with many more surely to come.

The "discovery" of giant footprints at Bluff Creek in 1958 that introduced Bigfoot to the American public spawned not only a spate of ongoing ape-man sightings over the years but also a variety of organizations whose goal is to educate people about the mystery beasts, conduct research about them, and act as their advocates.

One of the first organizations dedicated to Bigfoot was North American Wildlife Research, the group that built the Bigfoot trap in the southwestern Oregon forest in the 1970s. The organization's founder, Ron Olson, also co-wrote *Sasquatch: The Legend of Bigfoot,* a 1977 television docudrama that starred Eugene-area actors. In fact, Bigfoot has become so popular that interest—and sightings—have spread not only throughout America but to other countries as well.

Currently there are official Bigfoot organizations and researchers in at least eighteen states; a Bigfoot museum near Felton, California; and Bigfoot groups in Canada, Australia, and Russia. Jeffrey Meldrum, an associate professor of anatomy and anthropology at Idaho State University in Pocatello, has found suspected Bigfoot tracks and is even trying to develop Bigfoot research as a respectable academic pursuit.

Not only do Bigfoot true believers devour every piece of information about the hairy creature they can lay their hands on, but they also participate in field expeditions that are offered regularly by Bigfoot organizations.

But finding a Bigfoot isn't an easy task, and a careful strategy is required to optimize one's chance for success. Serious

Sasquatch searchers have even compiled some suggestions for planning an expedition. First and foremost, they recommend that you hook up with an established Bigfoot organization that has extensive field experience and sign up for a research expedition. In the company of experts, your odds will be much better than striking off on your own.

It's also important to do your research beforehand and concentrate your search in areas with the most recent Bigfoot sightings, on the assumption that those places harbor larger populations or that perhaps a nomadic band of the creatures is lingering there to be discovered. Serious Bigfoot researchers also need to make a serious time commitment and camp out for several days in Bigfoot country during the course of their expedition. Calling for Bigfoot by letting loose with frequent and loud "woooos" may prompt one within earshot to respond in kind. For those inclined to a more high-tech approach, motion- or infrared-activated cameras placed along forest trails may give the desired results. Bigfoot researchers not only hope for a sighting but also search for other evidence, such as hairs and tracks that might prove one of the creatures has been in the area. Lastly, the more time Bigfoot researchers spend in the woods and mountains, the more likely they are to eventually find one.

A typical Sasquatch search, organized by the Bigfoot Field Researchers Organization, was conducted in June 2007 in the Deschutes National Forest in central Oregon, one of the three top Bigfoot hot spots in the state. Several dozen Bigfoot aficionados searched the forested terrain day and night, howling in hopes of reciprocation, looking for signs such as tracks and scats, and hoping to glimpse one of the elusive creatures. Particularly indicative of a Bigfoot in the vicinity are sounds of sticks being struck against logs and trees, purported to be how the animals communicate. (It was these types of noises that led the forest geologist along the North Santiam River years ago to think that Bigfoot was shadowing him.) But this expedition, like most, turned up no solid evidence.

Nevertheless, as one of the top alleged Bigfoot territories, Deschutes County is a good place to conduct such a search. Two of the most significant Oregon Bigfoot sightings have occurred there, going back to the 1940s and 1950s. The first was in 1942, when Don Hunter and his wife were driving along the Cascade Lakes Highway, southwest of the city of Bend. As they neared the vicinity of Todd Lake, they were surprised to spot a large, hairy figure in a meadow alongside the road. Hunter pulled the car over to the shoulder, and he and his wife got out to have a better look. But as soon as they revealed themselves, the tall mystery creature ran off into the forest—on two legs. When the Hunters later related the details of their encounter to others, they were adamant that the thing they saw was bipedal and therefore could not have been a black bear. Because Hunter was a staff member of the University of Oregon at the time, his account was regarded as a credible observation.

The Deschutes County Bigfoot encounter a decade later was a more curious case. In this instance, a man named Zack

Hamilton claimed not only to have seen a Bigfoot deep in the wilderness surrounding the Three Sisters mountains but to have been stalked by the creature as well. He managed to take a few photos of his pursuer, dropped them off at a photography shop to be developed, but never returned to pick them up.

Most Deschutes County Bigfoot sightings are focused in the Cascade Mountains area, including the Three Sisters Wilderness Area, Todd Lake, and Newberry National Volcanic Monument.

If Bigfoot believers are eternally optimistic about the creature's existence, the chronic lack of solid evidence is not lost on Bigfoot skeptics, who point out the improbability that such large creatures can supposedly roam across a wide area in family groups without being seen more regularly, as are bears, mountain lions, and other secretive wild animals. A dead one has never been found. Attempts to identify suspected Bigfoot hair samples using DNA analysis have so far proved inconclusive. For scientists to accept Bigfoot as real, the only definitive evidence they will consider is a specimen, either dead or alive.

Hoaxes don't help the cause either. A case in point is Ray Wallace, of Mount Vernon, Oregon, who died on November 26, 2002. After his passing, relatives came forward with the astounding news that he, along with brother Wilbur, was behind the famous 1958 Bluff Creek Bigfoot footprints as well as the famous Patterson-Gimlin Bigfoot film footage. His relatives said that the two brothers constructed numerous Bigfoot "feet" of fiberglass, cement, and wood and used them to make the Bluff

Creek prints, along with many others, during three decades of travels throughout the Pacific Northwest. In addition, Wallace's relatives said that the famous Bigfoot film was of their great aunt Elna in a gorilla suit.

Bigfoot skeptics had long considered the Patterson-Gimlin film a hoax, although the two filmmakers swore it was genuine, and supporters argued that a close inspection shows muscle movement and shoulder blades flexing under skin in a way that could never be duplicated with a Hollywood monkey outfit. Moreover, supporters argue that, upon close examination, the footprints—which remain the best and most ubiquitous proof of Bigfoot's existence that believers have—show flexing of the mid-foot. This flexing is similar to a great ape's foot motion and is an anatomical characteristic that fake feet would not show.

So it's a stalemate. No one can prove that Bigfoot roams the wild mountains and forests of Oregon, but no one can prove that it doesn't. Just remember that the next time you camp in the woods and glimpse a hulking shadow in the brush, smell a nasty odor wafting in the wind, or hear what sounds like someone whacking sticks against the trees.

CHAPTER 3

THE BRIDGE OF THE GODS

It was October 1805, and the Lewis and Clark expedition was plying the reach of the Columbia River between Hood River and Eagle Creek. Although the explorers had no way of knowing it at the time, the mouth of the Columbia River and the Pacific Ocean lay just 150 miles downstream, and they would reach their long-sought destination within a couple of weeks. But for now, they were slowly making their way by canoe, recording scientific observations as they went per instructions of the expedition's sponsor, President Thomas Jefferson.

Ever alert to the surrounding environment, Captains Lewis and Clark noted an unusual phenomenon along this river stretch near the current city of Cascade Locks that Clark described as a "remarkable circumstance"—large numbers of tree stumps standing erect in the river, their trunks protruding well above the surface singly and in groups as if they had sprouted from the water's depths. Lewis and Clark also observed many large rocks that had the "appearance of having Separated from the mountains and fallen promiscuisly [*sic*] into the river." They surmised that this was evidence of a major landslide, which they estimated to have occurred about twenty years earlier. Lewis, after giving it some additional thought, later wrote in his journals that the presence of the trees and rocks might indicate that the Columbia River had been dammed by debris at some point in the past.

Unbeknownst to Lewis and Clark, they were looking at the last remaining clues pointing to a cataclysmic geological event in the Columbia River Gorge that spawned a host of Native American legends, which were grounded in reality and might even be tied to a geological event whose violent impacts reverberated across the Pacific Ocean to as far away as Japan—the Bridge of the Gods.

Years later, other white explorers and pioneers journeying down the Columbia River also encountered the mysterious concentration of stumps that came to be known as the "submerged forest of the Columbia" as well as Clark's promiscuously strewn rocks, which created the frothing water and navigational hazard called Cascade Rapids.

Those travelers expounded their own theories and opinions of these phenomena after seeing the evidence for themselves. Floating through the submerged forest in 1835, the missionary Reverend Samuel Parker rejected the landslide theory and postulated instead that the rocks and trees came to be in the river when a section of riverbank gradually caved in over a period of time. Missionaries Joseph Frost and Daniel Lee leaned more toward

G. K. GILBERT, U.S. GEOLOGICAL SURVEY

Cascade Rapids of the Columbia River, formed by the collapse of the Bridge of the Gods, as viewed in 1899.

Lewis and Clark's big landslide theory. In 1841, when the Wilkes Expedition passed through, observers felt that the trees and large rocks came to be in the river as the result of erosion of its banks caused by spring floods. The famed western explorer John C. Frémont visited this section of the river two years later and declared the landslide scenario to be the most likely.

The Native Americans who lived along the Columbia River had their own theory that explained the underwater forest and mighty rapids, expressed in various tribal legends. There are a number of variations, depending on which tribe tells the story, but they all go something like this: At one time, not too long

31

ago, where the Cascade mountain range meets the Columbia River, a great natural arch bridged the two shores, and tribes who lived on either side of the river regularly used it to cross back and forth. The bridge was called the Bridge of Tomaniwuas, after a spiritual deity who created it so that people could easily cross the river to visit and trade with each other. In the middle of the bridge lived an old witch-woman named Loowit, who kept guard over a fire that she would not share with anyone else, although people would often try to steal it from her.

Finally, weary of the constant pestering, Loowit asked Tomaniwuas for permission to give the people fire so they could cook food and warm themselves, which he gave. Then, because Loowit had always been such a faithful servant to Tomaniwuas, he offered to grant her one wish. She asked that he make her young and beautiful. Concerned that this might eventually lead to trouble, he nevertheless bestowed upon her youthful vigor and great beauty. It was to lead to more trouble than either imagined.

Upon gazing at the now-lovely Loowit, two chiefs—one named Klickitat, who ruled the tribe north of the river, and the other called Wyest, who presided over the south—fell inconsolably in love with her. Unable to make up her mind between the two, the angry and insulted headmen snubbed Loowit whenever they crossed the great bridge. This state of affairs eventually poisoned the relationship between the two tribes, and war broke out, resulting in much killing and destruction.

Infuriated by this turn of events caused by Loowit's wish, Tomaniwuas returned to Earth and killed her, along with Klickitat and Wyest. He then turned their bodies into Mount St. Helens, Mount Adams, and Mount Hood, respectively. But Tomaniwuas wasn't done yet. To keep the warring tribes apart, he vowed to destroy the bridge, sending a terrible storm that night. Amid the cracking lightning and roar of thunder, a tremendous fissure appeared in the riverbed, destroying the great bridge for all time and sending rocks and trees tumbling into the Columbia River. The submerged forest and the large rocks that created the tumultuous Cascade Rapids were all that remained of the mighty Bridge of Tomaniwuas. White settlers, explorers, and scientists dismissed native tales describing a "Bridge of the Gods" as nonsense.

A fascinating aspect of these native stories about the Bridge of the Gods stressed that these events occurred "not too long ago—perhaps five, six old [women] ago," suggesting just a few generations back at most. Indeed, in 1869 local tribal members told Thomas Condon, a missionary and later Oregon's first state geologist, that the Cascade Rapids were not very ancient and did not exist during the time of their fathers, when it was possible to canoe unimpeded from the sea to the falls at The Dalles. Once the five-mile-long rapids were formed, with a drop of thirty-seven feet, voyagers had to portage around them for safety.

For geologists, the Columbia River Gorge for its entire seventy-five-mile length is nothing less than a wonderland as the river flows along the Oregon-Washington border from The Dalles to Portland and bisecting the Cascade Range. Among nonscientists, the gorge is known for its beauty and especially for its magnificent gallery of waterfalls, with seventy-one falls within a 420-square-mile area, eleven of which are more than one hundred feet high.

Because of its beauty and scientific (especially geological) value, nearly 300,000 acres stretching for eighty-five miles on both sides of the river were designated the Columbia River Gorge National Scenic Area on November 17, 1986, to protect it from overdevelopment. Some of its major attractions include Rooster Rock, remnants of an ancient landslide; Crown Point, a chunk of lava that filled what was once a side canyon 14.5 million years ago; spectacular Multnomah Falls, the highest waterfall in the gorge at 620 feet; and Beacon Rock, a steep 800-foot-high vertical peak composed of lava and named by Lewis and Clark when they passed downriver on their way to the sea.

The geological story of the gorge is testimony to the relentless power of water. The gorge's ancient river channel was regularly blocked by gigantic lava flows seeking the easiest path downhill, blocked by landslides, and then scoured clean by floods of biblical proportion.

Sixteen million years ago, a series of massive basaltic lava flows made their way down the gorge, on their way to the Pacific Ocean, popping and sizzling as they went. As these flows hardened, they created dams that blocked the river. The waters of the

Columbia, as intent on reaching the sea as the lava, simply cut new channels to find its way. Over the millennia, when smaller flows intruded into the gorge, the river simply cut a new route through the rock.

Then geological Armageddon struck the Columbia River Gorge. The beginnings of this catastrophic event lay about two million years in the past during a series of Ice Ages, when great continental ice sheets covered the landscape of northern North America. Over time these ice sheets alternately advanced and retreated. During the course of this process, a great ice dam stretched from the Canadian border to the Clark's Fork River and turned much of what is now western Montana into a huge natural reservoir that held vast amounts of water. (Geologists call the ancient lake Lake Missoula. It no longer exists.) Between 15,500 and 13,000 years ago, the ice dam periodically breached and then re-formed, creating a series of floods of fantastic proportions that sent an unimaginable amount of water, ragged chunks of ice, and debris roaring down the river's channel and sweeping aside not just boulders, trees, and other objects on the land, but the very land itself.

It was an unstoppable force that has been estimated to have traveled at nine cubic miles per hour for forty hours. A typical Missoulian flood was composed of about four hundred cubic miles of water, more than the total flow of all the rivers in the world for a year. Flooding the Columbia's tributaries to depths of up to four hundred feet as it rushed to the Pacific Ocean, the water carved out the steep walls of the Columbia River Gorge that visitors see today.

While the gorge's native inhabitants had their explanation for the submerged forest and Cascade Rapids and early travelers had theirs, it wasn't until the mid-1850s that professional geologists started to take an interest in the mystery conjured up by the intrepid Lewis and Clark.

The professionals, too, had a range of explanations. John Newberry, a member of the 1854–1855 Pacific Railroad Survey, reported that the sunken forest was formed when recent volcanic activity caused the river to be partially blocked and flooded the forest adjacent to the river. In 1870 another geologist proposed that the flowing river carved a hole in the riverbed, causing the entire river to flow underground for some distance before re-emerging. Eventually this underground tunnel collapsed, damming the river.

But it wasn't until 1916 that geologist Ira A. Williams put his finger on what was becoming the suspected true explanation for the submerged forest of the Columbia and Cascade Rapids, with its boulders much too large for the river current to have washed from somewhere upstream. There really had been a Bridge of the Gods.

Over the next twenty years, more research went into this stretch of the river and gorge in preparation for the construction of Bonneville Dam between 1934 and 1938 at river mile 146. During the course of those studies, geologists ascertained that the theory of a great landslide that dammed the river and created the fabled bridge was indeed correct. They named it the Bonneville Landslide.

The first attempt to scientifically and systematically examine the submerged forest and Cascade Rapids to determine their age—and therefore the age of the Bonneville Landslide—came when Portland resident Donald B. Lawrence, a doctoral student at Johns Hopkins University, tallied, photographed, mapped, and measured the underwater forest during low-water periods of 1934 and 1935. From the data he gleaned from his study of the submerged trees, along with what was already known about the Bonneville Landslide, emerged a likely scenario of an event that, if not exactly in accordance with Native American tales, was equally violent.

Sometime in the distant past, as the Columbia River altered its channel when lava flows blocked its previous path, the river flowed up against 3,400-foot-high walls of the gorge's north side, topped by old basalt 1,500 feet deep, about 30 miles upstream from present-day Portland. The relentless waters of the Columbia, which no ancient flow of molten rock could ever deter, quietly and steadily worked its will until one day it had eroded the rocky cliffs enough to cause a collapse. Massive chunks of what today are known as Table Mountain and Greenleaf Peak came roaring down into the river in a swirling cauldron of soil, boulders, and uprooted trees.

The slide itself, located about thirty miles east of Portland just west of Cascade Locks, was five and a half square miles in size. It hit the river with such force that it plowed all the way to the south shore, effectively creating an earthen dam two hundred to three hundred feet high that halted the Columbia's march to the sea. The river water slowly began to gather and pool behind this new obstruction, flooding the upstream forest for as much as twenty-five miles.

At its peak, Lawrence estimated the impoundment to have been as much as 90 miles long, covering 88 square miles, and containing up to 5.2 million acre-feet of water. Because it stretched from shore to shore and was about three and a half miles wide, it could very well have served as a crossing for humans living and traveling along the river. The oral histories of tribes living in the region suggest that was the case.

How long before water won the unevenly matched battle with earth is hard to say for certain, but the bridge did not endure for long. It lasted long enough to deposit twenty-five feet of sediment around the sunken trees on the upstream side of the riverbed. The dam may have collapsed violently after a rush of high water from spring snowmelt, flowing and gathering strength from the Columbia's many high-elevation tributaries. At best, it lasted until the rising water behind the dam reached the top of the obstruction, breaching it in the process. At current river flow rates, that process is estimated to have taken anywhere from a couple of months to two years.

However long it finally took, the unimaginable power of all that pent-up water—roughly 1.7 trillion gallons of it—forcing

G. K. GILBERT, U.S. GEOLOGICAL SURVEY

Tree stumps of the sunken forest in the Columbia River, as viewed in 1899.

itself through a breach in the dam tore immense rocks loose and scattered them downstream, carving a steeper gradient in the process and creating a large and violent set of rapids strewn with massive boulders. The mighty Bridge of the Gods was gone— forged by the cataclysmic forces of the earth, it was destroyed by those same powers.

But when did this happen? The silent, waterlogged trees sprouting from the Columbia still held secrets to be revealed. Working with 1930s scientific technology, Lawrence took growth-ring samples from a selection of sunken trees. The old- est tree he found was 260 years old, which he calculated to have been killed at least 200 years earlier, or about 70 years before the

Lewis and Clark expedition encountered the submerged forest. That put the date of the Bonneville Landslide and the Bridge of the Gods in the mid-1730s.

Lawrence's further study of the submerged trees revealed a few other prime pieces of information. A significant portion of the submerged forest was made up of Douglas fir trees, a species whose roots are intolerant of too much water and which generally grows where groundwater is not too shallow. Their presence suggested that those trees, when they were alive, grew away from the riverbank, beyond the high-water zone, and probably did not end up in the river via a temporary flood but rather were inundated in a large pool or reservoir. That linked them to the Bonneville Landslide and the Bridge of the Gods. It also suggested that the steep gradient of the Cascade Rapids did not exist when the trees were engulfed by the rising water that turned the river into lake.

Two decades later, with the development of radiocarbon dating, Lawrence had some of his old tree samples tested. The results showed that the trees had been submerged around 1250. Later, improved testing procedures of those samples put the date at 1450.

But the Bonneville Landslide and the Bridge of the Gods continue to intrigue scientists, and ongoing research just intensifies the mystery. In the late 1990s an old, half-buried Douglas fir log from remnants of the Bonneville Landslide was dated with radiocarbon testing. The tree was determined to have died between 1500 and 1760. A tree-ring count showed that it had died in 1699. A few years later, a researcher with the U.S. Forest Service, using the known growth rate of certain species of lichen to determine how old their host is, found that the trees taken from the landslide area had died sometime between 1670 and 1760.

That new information brought some exciting implications. First, the slide and the bridge may have been younger than previously thought, putting them in the period that Native Americans in the 1800s described as "the time of our fathers." Second, it places the slide and the bridge in the general time frame of, and potentially links them to, one of the Pacific Northwest's other great cataclysmic geological events—the Cascadia earthquake.

On the morning of January 26, 1700, a devastating earthquake, estimated to have measured up to 9.2 on the Richter scale, originated in the Pacific Ocean off the West Coast of North America between Vancouver Island and northern California. The tremendous forces generated by restless tectonic plates beneath the ocean sent shockwaves emanating throughout the region and beyond. The earthquake is believed to have caused a tsunami that struck Japan over the next few days, flooding coastlines and destroying houses and other property. If the newer dates for the deaths of the submerged forest trees hold true, then the Bonneville Landslide and the creation of the Bridge of the Gods may have been triggered by the Cascadia earthquake of 1700, just 105 years before Lewis and Clark came across the drowned firs and cedars.

The Sherlock Holmeses of geology continue their detective work, hoping to someday discover the final truth of the Bridge of the Gods, which once briefly spanned the mighty Columbia River. But fresh evidence is hard to come by. Most of the area where the bridge once stood, along with Cascade Rapids, is forever submerged beneath the pool that formed when Bonneville Dam went into operation in 1938.

Just as it was when Lewis and Clark passed through on their way to the sea, the Columbia River Gorge still bustles with people. In Lewis and Clark's time, Native American tribes thrived along its banks, living off the river's abundant salmon runs and trading goods with neighboring tribes. Today, small towns are scattered up and down the gorge, and thousands of tourists come year-round to see its natural wonders. And believe it or not, a traveler can cross the Bridge of the Gods.

In 1926 construction of a $650,000, 1,856-foot-long truss cantilever bridge, about four miles upstream from Bonneville Dam, was completed. It was named after the natural bridge that once crossed the river in the general area—the Bridge of the Gods.

But travelers crossing the Bridge of the Gods today won't encounter old Loowit faithfully guarding her sacred fire. Instead, they are confronted by a tollbooth and pay $1 to pass to the other side.

CHAPTER 4

THE PORT ORFORD METEORITE MYSTERY

At some point in the unimaginably distant past, the huge rock broke off from one of the asteroids orbiting in a belt between Mars and Jupiter and began tumbling through the solar system at tremendous speed as it charted its own path around the sun. After millions of years, planet Earth crossed its trajectory, and the rock slammed into its atmosphere. Unlike in the vacuum of space, the pressure and friction of Earth's gaseous shroud caused the rock to erupt into a fireball. Most pieces of space debris that penetrate the planet's atmosphere disintegrate before they reach the surface and are called meteors by astronomers. But some of these wayward space objects survive the terrible heat generated from their fall and slam into the Earth's surface. Those survivors are called meteorites, and this particular space rock was a meteorite that lit up the sky over present-day Port Orford, Oregon, where it crashed into the side of a nearby mountain with such force that it almost completely buried itself in the ground.

43

At least that is what some believe, and since the Port Orford Meteorite was first "discovered" in 1856, hundreds of believers have fruitlessly scoured the forests and mountains east of its namesake town for the heavenly object purported to be worth millions of dollars. Others believe the fabled visitor from space was merely a prop in an audacious scam by a desperate scientist to con the U.S. Congress into paying debts he owed for out-of-control research expenses and frontier real estate speculation gone bad.

The story begins with Dr. John Evans, an explorer and geologist who worked for the U.S. government. Evans was born in 1812 in Portsmouth, New Hampshire. His father was an associate justice of the state's Superior Court, and his mother was the great-granddaughter of Samuel Penhollow, a prominent figure in the early settlement and governance of colonial New Hampshire. He eventually married and in 1839 moved to St. Louis, Missouri, with his wife, three sons, and a daughter. Evans attended medical school, although there is some question as to whether he ever obtained a degree. Nevertheless, he came to be known over time as Dr. Evans, whether he earned the title or not.

Whatever his formal education, by 1847 he had found work as a field geologist on an expedition to survey the geological resources of Wisconsin, Minnesota, Iowa, and the Nebraska Territory. Two years later, during the course of his travels, he found a mother lode of fossils in the Badlands of South Dakota. This discovery enhanced his reputation enough as a scientist to land him an appointment to explore the geology of the Oregon

JIM YUSKAVITCH

*According to John Evans, a 22,000-pound pallasite meteorite worth
millions of dollars lies hidden somewhere in the coastal mountains
east of Port Orford.*

Territory under the auspices of the Department of the Inte-
rior. This enterprise, financed by the U.S. Congress, explored,
mapped, and documented the territory's geology on the western
side of the Cascade Mountains over several trips between 1851
and 1856. On his final expedition in 1856, he visited the Port
Orford area and other parts of the southern Oregon coast.

Evans had been turning over the minerals he collected on
his Oregon excursions to one Dr. A. Litton for further study.
Unfortunately, Litton's wife died in 1858, and the doctor
informed Evans that her loss weighed on him so greatly that he

could no longer concentrate on his work and that Evans would need to find another scientist to examine his specimens. By that time, Litton had completed work on all the mineral samples that Evans had sent him. But Evans engaged the scientific services of Boston chemist Dr. Charles T. Jackson and provided him additional specimens for analysis. Before long, Jackson made a stunning discovery among the specimens that sat silently on his laboratory table and brought it to the attention of the scientific world at the October 5, 1859, meeting of the Boston Society of Natural History.

Jackson claimed that among the samples that Dr. John Evans had brought back from the southern Oregon coast was a piece of a meteorite. While a meteorite is always an exciting find for geologists, this was not just any meteorite. According to Dr. Jackson's investigations, the Port Orford Meteorite, as it became known, was a type of meteorite called a pallasite. Pallasites, which make up only 1 percent of all the meteorites found on the planet, are composed of iron-nickel and embedded with olivine crystals that are sometimes gem quality. In the published meeting proceedings of the Boston Society of Natural History, Dr. Jackson compared it to the famous 1,500-pound pallasite that was discovered in Siberia in 1772, a period in history when science was skeptical of the idea of rocks from space hitting the earth.

Jackson sent off a small sample of the meteorite to Vienna to have his work confirmed by independent scientists, who verified that it was, indeed, a pallasite. He also began corresponding with Dr. Evans to inform him of his findings and to determine if Evans could pinpoint exactly where the specimen came from.

In a letter of reply, Evans confidently assured Jackson there would be no difficulty in finding the entire meteorite, which he estimated at about 22,000 pounds when he hammered off his samples. The world's largest pallasite was embedded on the west face of a peak called Bald Mountain, protruding about three feet aboveground, approximately thirty or thirty-five miles from the small seaport town of Port Orford. He could easily go back and retrieve the entire meteorite; however, because of the rugged and mountainous nature of the landscape, which was accessible only by primitive trail, it would probably have to be broken into pieces ranging from 100 to 150 pounds and packed out by mules. Evans calculated the cost of hauling the meteorite out piecemeal at between $1,200 and $1,500—an excellent value considering how much it would be worth to science.

Evans proposed organizing an expedition to Bald Mountain and bringing back this great scientific find. Jackson was all for it, noting that the meteorite not only had monetary and scientific value but also was a national treasure that should not fall into the hands of a foreign collector, museum, or government. All that was required was to procure funding for the proposed expedition.

To that end, Drs. Evans and Jackson began contacting colleagues in the scientific community and at various institutes of higher learning and urged them to use their influence to sway Congress into financing a recovery expedition to the mountains east of Port Orford, Oregon. But money was not forthcoming. The Smithsonian, which Jackson had corresponded with to suggest it should underwrite the venture, was cool to the idea; moreover, funds were tight in Washington, D.C., in general as growing tensions between the North and the South threatened to erupt into all-out war. Jackson and Evans's repeated attempts to entice the federal government to reach into the public purse for a recovery mission made no headway.

In 1860 Evans landed a position as a geologist on a U.S. Navy expedition to the Isthmus of Panama to assess the extent and value of the coal deposits in the region. He returned to the United States in early 1861, still hopeful of raising government funds to return to Bald Mountain. But it was not to be. Just forty-nine years old, he died of pneumonia on April 13, 1861, the day after Confederate troops fired on Fort Sumter, marking the beginning of the Civil War.

With a war on, the idea of searching for a distant, lost meteorite, regardless of how valuable it might be, faded. The three known specimens languished in museums: one sample at the Boston Society of Natural History (it was acquired by the Smithsonian Institution in 1920); another piece in Vienna; and the third in Calcutta.

Nevertheless, while the government had given up on the meteorite, the rumor mill remained alive and well as word spread that a monstrously large and valuable rock from outer space lay somewhere deep in the mountains near Port Orford.

Then, in 1917, a New Orleans anthropologist named David Bushnell came across one of Dr. Evans's old journals, "Route from Port Orford across the Rogue River Mountains," the very portion of the doctor's writings that would show the way to the fabled pallasite. Bushnell located one of Evans's sons and gave him the journal; the son in turn donated it to the Smithsonian. Bushnell happened to have a friend in Washington, D.C., with connections, and finally, in 1929, the Smithsonian agreed to look for the Port Orford Meteorite. The museum dispatched its director of mineralogy and petrology, W. F. Foshag, to the wild Oregon mountains. He returned empty-handed.

But meteorite fever was gripping the region as word of the Smithsonian expedition went out. The *Portland Oregonian* newspaper published speculative accounts that the pallasite was worth as much as $2.2 million, based on $100 per pound that some collectors paid for rare meteorite samples, and false rumors swirled that the Smithsonian was offering a generous reward for even small pieces of the space rock.

During the 1930s hundreds of people combed the mountains east of Port Orford in search of the treasure. For some, it was a serious and solemn endeavor, while for others it was a holiday lark. True believers among the private citizenry even formed the Society for the Recovery of the Lost Port Orford Meteorite to organize search parties. The Smithsonian was so swamped by requests for copies of Evans's journal and other information from would-be meteorite discoverers that the institution finally produced a brief information sheet that it sent in response to those inquiries.

One intriguing story to arise during the heyday of the search for the meteorite revolves around Bob Harrison, a miner from Myrtle Point, which lies along the banks of the Coquille River near the coast. One day sometime in the late 1930s, he announced that not only did he know where the meteorite was, but he also owned it since it lay within one of his mining claims along a stream called Poverty Creek. From his description of the area, the claim was thought to be near either Barklow Mountain or Granite Butte in either Coos or Curry County.

While digging around on his claim in search of nickel deposits, he said he found the meteorite, chipped off a piece, and sent it to the U.S. Geological Survey, where it was examined by Dr. J. F. Diller. Diller declared the sample to be a meteorite fragment and wrote back to Harrison, encouraging him to send a sample to the Smithsonian Institution for more thorough study.

Based on Diller's conclusions, Harrison reported that he also sent off a sample to the Oregon state geological office in Grants Pass for further confirmation and gave a number of interviews to newspaper reporters on the subject of his discovery. Since interest in the Port Orford Meteorite was then running high, his story received quite a bit of play in the newspapers.

But the samples he claimed to have sent to the state geological laboratory never arrived, and soon after the flush of publicity, Harrison ceased claiming that he had the famous rock. Whether tests eventually revealed his samples not to have been from a meteorite or whether he made it all up for the publicity isn't clear. But Harrison vanished from the public eye without ever offering an explanation or further proof of his claimed discovery.

In the summer of 1939, the Smithsonian sent another expedition to Oregon under the leadership of E. P. Henderson, associate curator of the Division of Meteorites, who attempted to retrace Evans's route in the Port Orford area by following the directions in his journal. Although he was able to trace Evans's general 1856 route, the journal was ultimately unhelpful in finding the alleged location of the lost Port Orford Meteorite, and he, too, returned home unsuccessful.

Despite the complete failure of all efforts to find the meteorite (and the somewhat inexact nature of Dr. Evans's directions to Bald Mountain), the searches continued. By the mid-1960s, hopeful prospectors had been looking for their treasure for at least fifty years, and even then thirty or forty people per year were still combing the area looking for Bald Mountain. Also by then, many scientists—including the Smithsonian's E. P. Henderson, who had tried to find the meteorite himself—were beginning to have serious doubts that it really existed.

A number of factors raised suspicions about the story's veracity. Evans never mentioned a meteorite in his journals; his later description of the pallasite's location was unclear; and many mountains in the Port Orford region met the general criteria of its supposed resting place. Also, the authenticity of the samples was coming under question. And adding to the intrigue, it turned out that the doctor was in debt from his previous expeditions and for city lots he bought during his trips to the Oregon Territory, fueling a theory that the whole meteorite tale was a con game designed to settle those liabilities courtesy of the U.S. taxpayer.

An examination of Dr. Evans's expedition journal brought the first doubts. The surviving journal appears to have been written or transcribed by someone other than Evans on unbound paper with some sections missing. Although many have closely examined the document over the years, there is no mention of the meteorite. It was a curious omission considering the scientific value of such a find, which would surely have merited a significant write-up in the expedition's official records and observations.

When Dr. Charles Jackson first corresponded with Evans regarding the pallasite samples, Evans claimed that the meteorite could be readily located, and he eventually produced a description of the place where he claimed it lay. According to Evans, it was situated on the "western face of Bald Mountain." The mountain, which he described as about thirty-five miles from the coast and a prominent landmark, had a smooth, grassy slope with no trees. Unfortunately, his description fit any number of mountains in the area, many of which had treeless summits and were commonly called Bald Mountain by local residents.

In the mid-1980s Howard Plotkin, of the University of Western Ontario, made an extensive study of Evans's claims. He then produced a monograph called *The Port Orford, Oregon*

Meteorite Mystery, which presented evidence arguing against the pallasite's existence and bolstering claims that the whole affair was a hoax.

After a careful study of Evans's 1856 journal describing his travels in the Rogue River Mountains near Port Orford, Plotkin concluded that Johnson Mountain best met the criteria as the location of the lost meteorite. He based his conclusion on the geographic data that Evans gave in his letters to Jackson and by matching that information to landmarks, distance from the coast, and overall terrain. In 1986 and 1987, Plotkin and a companion thoroughly searched the mountain and adjacent ridgelines using a proton magnetometer, which measures magnetic intensity. Since pallasites have a high iron-nickel content, they have significant magnetic properties that make the magnetometer the instrument most likely to detect a pallasite, especially if it is completely buried. After two field seasons of searching, they found nothing but occasional occurrences of normal levels of magnetic activity.

The origin of the samples that Dr. Jackson identified as part of a larger pallasite was also coming under fire. Analysis of the samples showed they had a "fusion crust"—a glassy coating that envelops a meteor as it cools—and that its metal content was unbattered and the olivine crystals were in good condition. This suggested that the meteorite samples were not removed from a larger mass, which would have required a great deal of hammering, causing telltale damage. One theory claims that the pallasite samples Evans gave to Jackson were in fact specimens of the Imilac meteorite that he had acquired on his trip across the Isthmus of Panama in 1858, while returning home from Oregon after attending to his business interests there.

Indians discovered the Imilac meteorite in Chile while out hunting sometime in the early 1820s. Over the next few years, many samples of that pallasite—only the third pallasite to have been found at that point in time—had been distributed to museums throughout the world. Someone who knew his way around those institutions probably could have purchased a sample without too much difficulty. But why would Evans "seed" his Oregon geological samples with a meteorite from Chile?

Plotkin postulated that it had to do with money. Although Congress had appropriated funds for his geological expeditions to Oregon, he was prone to cost overruns. By the time he had completed his final 1856 trip, he was saddled with a personal debt of just over $11,000. In addition, during the course of his visits, Evans had purchased lots in Oregon City, hoping to sell them later at a great profit. But a glut in available land lowered prices and depressed sales. Because he was unable to sell his property, his real estate debt with interest mounted, reaching more than $1,000. The value of his lots eventually decreased by half.

According to the hoax theory, Evans concocted the meteorite story as a way to spur the federal government into financing another expedition to Oregon. He would then be able to divert some of the funds to retire his financial obligations. To get the scheme started, he sent Dr. Jackson a sample of a valuable and extremely rare type of meteorite that came from South America, not the Oregon Territory, which he procured after his final Oregon expedition. And that's why his journals never mentioned the meteorite's discovery—because he hadn't thought of the scheme yet.

Dr. Evans has his defenders. They argue that his debt was much less than detractors claim and that he was reimbursed for his cost overruns, which were all legitimate. Therefore, they claim, he had no need to concoct a plan to defraud the government with tales of a nonexistent meteorite.

Some of his defenders place part of the blame on Dr. Jackson, who may have had some problems with alcohol and mental fitness, along with a reputation for sloppy scientific work. It is possible that he inadvertently mixed other pallasite specimens from his collection (which reportedly included some Imilac meteorite pieces) in with the Port Orford samples, thereby confusing the situation.

Some people also allege that the Smithsonian mishandled some specimens purported to be the Port Orford Meteorite. In 1861 Dr. Jackson reportedly cut a sample from a larger sample of the meteorite for the purpose of donating it to the Imperial Mineralogical Museum in Vienna at the request of Austrian mineralogist Wilhelm Haidinger. In 1986 the Austrian specimen was loaned to the Smithsonian, providing an opportunity to compare it with a piece of the Port Orford Meteorite already in its possession, which had been acquired in 1920 from the Boston Society of Natural History.

Critics have alleged that the Smithsonian botched an opportunity to compare the two specimens to verify that they both came from the same specimen, which would have bolstered Evans's and Jackson's claims of the meteorite's authenticity. But the Smithsonian, Evans's defenders contend, did not adequately document the physical characteristics of its sample before dissecting it, making it difficult or impossible to match it with the Vienna sample obtained directly from Dr. Jackson.

Although there are still believers in the Port Orford Meteorite, the rush to find it has ebbed. Is there a ten-ton pallasite meteorite embedded with gem-quality olivine buried somewhere on the open slope of a treeless mountain peak in southern Oregon? Or is it the star player in a hoax to bilk the federal government? Who is to say? The only sure proof of its existence is to find it, but the mere fact that no one yet has done so does not mean it isn't there. By now the historical records, correspondence, journals, and chemical analysis may have revealed all they have to say about the lost Port Orford Meteorite. Now, perhaps the only way Dr. John Evans and his reputation will be restored is if someday a wanderer on some grassy height about thirty-five miles from Port Orford notices an unnatural mound and, scraping off the shallow layer of soil and vegetation, reveals a much larger mass made of stony iron and flecked with shards of green.

CHAPTER 5

THE LOST BLUE BUCKET MINE

how me the grave of the woman, and I'll show you bucketfuls of gold." That terse and somber admonition explains, so
it is said, the location of one of the legendary mother lodes of
western lore—Oregon's Lost Blue Bucket Mine. But before setting out into the eastern Oregon wilderness to find the lost mine
and claim its riches of gold, it behooves all would-be treasure
seekers to first learn who the woman in the grave is and how she
came to be there.

The story of the Lost Blue Bucket Mine begins on August
23, 1845, at Fort Boise, in what is now the state of Idaho. After
many months of arduous travel by wagon across the Great
Plains, followed by the rigors of the High Desert passage through
the Continental Divide, a party of 480 wagons carrying about
four thousand pioneers had stopped to rest, make repairs to
their wagons, and reprovision at this waypoint along the Oregon
Trail. These people, part of the great migration of settlers who
began crossing the continent from the eastern and midwestern

United States beginning in 1839, were heading for the promised land of the Oregon Territory. Their creaking wagons, holding the settlers' few belongings and all of their dreams, were pulled by teams of oxen but were driven by the universal human desire for a new home and a better life. Social and economic conditions played a motivational role as well. Times were hard in the late 1830s, especially in the Midwest. The economy was in a depression, and diseases were widespread, including cholera, typhoid, scarlet fever, malaria, diphtheria, and tuberculosis. In 1837 crop prices and farm values had crashed, the result of a series of floods that washed away farmlands and precipitated crop failures. Farm foreclosures were rampant.

With such economic and social unrest at home, the thought of crossing the continent, and all the hardship and suffering it entailed, sounded less daunting to many compared to the difficulties they would continue to endure if they stayed where they were. The first group of settlers to pack their wagons and set out for the Oregon Territory, establishing what would become known as the Oregon Trail, left Peoria, Illinois, in May 1839. Their successful arrival in Oregon's Willamette Valley helped open the floodgate of emigrants who followed them by the thousands to the trail's end to populate western Oregon and California.

The group of wagoneers camped at Fort Boise on that August night in 1845 was simply part of that wave of settlers who were destined to become part of western history. On that night they had reason to be happy, for they were about to embark on the last leg of a difficult journey that would take them to their new home in Oregon.

From Fort Boise, the final stretch of the now well-established Oregon Trail would take them west across the Snake River, north through the Blue Mountains of northeastern Oregon, and then west down the Columbia River, through the Cas-

Stephen Meek

CROOK COUNTY HISTORICAL SOCIETY

cade Mountains to the rich agricultural lands of the Willamette Valley. This final section was well known, safe, and generally took about twenty days to complete.

Even with the finish line in sight, another twenty days, after so many weeks on the trail, must have seemed like twenty too many. So when the Reverend Elijah White, who was making his way back east on business, stopped at Fort Boise and chatted with some of the bone-weary wagoneers, it may have appeared to them a gift of providence. The good reverend, it seems, had heard from reliable sources, of course, that there was a much shorter route to the Willamette Valley; it lay due west, straight across the Oregon desert, and would save them a week or more of travel time. As news of this "shortcut" spread through the camp, one Stephen Meek—brother of Joseph Meek, famed mountain man and key political figure in Oregon's inauguration into statehood in 1859—stepped forward and declared that he was familiar with the route and would act as a guide for the reasonable price of $5 per wagon.

The offer spread like wildfire among the wagon trains. Not only was there a shortcut to their new home, but there was also a man among them who knew the way. The pros and cons were discussed among the travelers and their families, and finally about eight hundred people in two hundred wagons elected to take Meek up on his offer.

In fact, however, the only thing Stephen Meek knew about this shortcut through the Oregon desert was a look at a map (which eventually proved to be highly inaccurate) that his brother Joe had helped produce while a member of a U.S. Army surveying expedition in 1841. He had never actually traveled that country himself. Why Meek decided to guide a wagon train through lands that he had never laid eyes on remains a mystery. Perhaps it was just a case of opportunism, the chance to make a good deal of extra money, along with the confidence that he could find the way without much difficulty and no one would be the wiser. Unfortunately, it was to prove a serious—and fatal—mistake for his naive clients. They were about to embark on what would become one of the epic stories of the settling of the American West and an enduring legend of treasure to boot.

The next day, August 24, the party started out. Initially, things went as expected, and progress was no more difficult than the earlier part of their journey. After two weeks of travel, they reached the Wagontire Mountains (southwest of present-day Burns) when things started taking a turn for the worse. Water was becoming a scarce commodity, and people were beginning to sicken and die. By mid-September the wagon train had reached a place called the Sinks of Lost Creek, where a small stream disappeared into the ground. The situation was becoming desperate. It was here that, according to wagon train member Samuel Hancock, a hundred men were sent out into the desert to find water. Seven days later they returned empty-handed.

By now it was apparent that Meek did not know where he was or how to get to the Willamette Valley. An angry confrontation ensued, and a majority voted to hang him, using raised wagon tongues as scaffolding since no suitable trees were available. Meek narrowly escaped this impromptu frontier justice when a sympathetic pioneer family hid him and his wife in their wagon until tempers cooled.

Finally realizing they were on their own, the pioneers had to make some hard decisions. What to do next? How to find their way out of the wilderness to the promised land, for which they had endured so much hardship to reach and which now seemed lost to them? Discussion and prayer would lead them to the proper decision. After much of both, the consensus was to divide into two groups and make for The Dalles, an outpost on the Oregon Trail along the Columbia River, and from there follow the established route to the Willamette Valley. The two groups struck out into the unknown wilderness of desert, forest, and mountains, maintaining a generally northerly course toward the Columbia River.

Forty-six days after departing from Fort Boise, the "Lost Meek Wagon Train" arrived at The Dalles, with straggler wagons arriving as much as a week later, completing what was one of the West's epic pioneer journeys. In all, the "shortcut" took more than twice as long as the Oregon Trail would have taken them. During the course of traveling the Meek Cut-Off, the pioneers left at least thirty-two of their number behind in lonely wilderness graves, one of whom was Mrs. Serepta King Chambers—the "woman in the grave" who shows the way to the Lost Blue Bucket Mine.

The story of how the Blue Bucket gold vein was discovered varies, but the traditional story has it that one day the party came to a stream flowing through a narrow gulch. The gulch was too tight a squeeze for the wagons to pass, so they went over a nearby hill to a better crossing, while the company's cattle were driven across the gulch. As the men were herding the animals to the other side of the small creek, a group of young girls amused themselves by wandering and playing along the banks. As they looked into the water and along the banks of the stream, they noticed some bright yellow rocks scattered about. Curiosity

CROOK COUNTY HISTORICAL SOCIETY

A wagon train carrying settlers west during the late 1800s, similar to that of the Lost Meek Wagon Train.

aroused, they began picking them up until they had collected twenty or thirty pounds of the pretty objects, which they placed in a wooden water bucket that was painted blue.

At camp that evening, the girls picked through their newly acquired rock collection, pounding some of the pieces flat against wagon tires. The adults also were curious about this mystery metal. But being farmers, not miners, they did not recognize gold "in the rough" and came to the conclusion that, though pretty, the rocks were worthless. With that, most of the strange metal was discarded. But one of its discoverers, thirteen years old at the time, took the largest piece, broke off the rock from the metal, and put it in her trunk in the family wagon. Several years after reaching the Willamette Valley, she settled down and married, and her name was now Mrs. Chapman. Still not knowing the rocks were gold, she reportedly had some of the large nuggets made into jewelry and used the remaining chunk as a doorstop. When her brother, who had gone off to the California goldfields after the big strike of 1849, returned home for a visit, he identified the mystery metal as gold. Moreover, the fact that she had to chip rock off the gold when she found it in the stream indicated that the source—the vein—was not far from where the nuggets were discovered.

There are other versions of how the nuggets were discovered. According to one story, Indians stole some horses from the group, and five or six pioneers struck out on horseback to overtake the thieves and retrieve the valuable animals. After riding seven or eight miles, they came upon a narrow gorge through which flowed a small creek consisting of a series of pools. Stopping to drink from the pools, they noticed many small yellow rocks in the creek bottom. They gathered them up and brought them back to camp, where they were examined by wagon train member Samuel Parker, who identified the nuggets as gold.

Another story relates that as J. W. Herren and his sister Susan were playing along a stream while their mother washed clothes, they found the gold, which Susan put in a blue bucket. Still another story says that twenty-one-year-old party member Dan Herren found the gold in some muddy cow tracks along the trail. Some tellings of the story have the gold lost before the settlers made it to their destination. But in all these different stories of the gold's discovery, there is one constant: After the rocks are positively identified as gold, the finders are unable to remember exactly where they found it. Eventually, some of the Meek party members recalled the gold being discovered sometime within a day or two of the death of Mrs. Chambers, who had wandered away during a wagon crossing of the Malheur River and succumbed on September 3, 1845, although none of the pioneers' journals recorded exactly what caused her demise. She was buried along the river. Although this information provided a critical clue and point of reference, to find the gold you would first have to find the grave, and to find the grave you would somehow have to retrace the lost wagon train's route. And to further confuse matters, it wasn't clear whether the gold was found a couple of days *before* or *after* Mrs. Chambers died. Nevertheless, that was more than enough information to motivate prospectors of the day, as gold fever had begun to infect Oregon in the 1850s.

The first known expedition to search for the "Blue Bucket Mine," as it came to be known, set out in 1851 armed with route information gleaned from some people who had been members of the lost wagon train. The group made it to Wagontire Mountain and found ample proof—in the form of abandoned belongings, equipment, broken wagon wheels, and graves—that the ill-fated travelers had passed here. But as far as gold was concerned, they came up empty-handed.

Another group—led by Benjamin Herron, who had actually been with the wagon train in 1845—headed out in 1854 with a plan to backtrack the original route. Eventually they encamped on the south fork of Pine Creek, where the lost wagon train had camped on September 5, 1845. This would have put them within a couple of days' journey of Mrs. Chambers's final resting place and close to the mother lode, according to the stories. But their hopes of riches were foiled when Indians attacked their camp, killed two of their number, and relieved them of their horses. The four survivors limped back home on foot.

Three years later, Dr. James McBride—another veteran of the Lost Meek Wagon Train, who had ended up in Yreka, California—led a party of seven in quest of the mine. His group managed to find the old trail in several places, marked by deep wagon-wheel ruts, but eventually lost it for good and finally had to give up. McBride tried again a year later with similar results.

One expedition of note was a party of fifty men led by George W. Bunch. In hopes of finding the fabled mine, they journeyed into the outback in 1860. Making it to the Wagon-tire Mountains, this group was able to successfully retrace much of the lost wagon train's travels. But a bad omen was, literally, in the air in the form of Indian smoke signals that the party had been noting as they traveled. Then one day the Indians attacked their camp, charging the prospectors while waving deer hides and howling in order to panic the horses into stampeding. After about an hour and two separate attacks, the Indians retreated, taking all the expedition's horses with them. This party, too, returned home goldless. Ironically, the Bunch expedition was camped on the south fork of Pine Creek when the attack occurred, the same location where the Herron party had been attacked six years earlier.

Even hucksters got into the game. In 1861 a man by the name of Adams claimed to have found evidence of gold on the Malheur River—where Mrs. Chambers reportedly died and was buried—and hawked his story on the streets of Portland until he had recruited a party of seventy prospectors. But, like the wagon train guide Stephen Meek, he only managed to get his men hopelessly lost in the desert. And, like Meek, he narrowly escaped a lynching by his furious compatriots. Instead, he was turned loose into the wilderness, where he eventually managed to join another party of miners who were working the goldfields of the Powder River country.

Over the years other groups have unsuccessfully attempted to retrace the route, often ending up many miles from where the lost wagon train's wheels ever rolled. The grave of Mrs. Chambers and the Blue Bucket Mine remained as lost as the Meek wagon train had been decades earlier.

Then, in 1877, came a breakthrough of sorts. The war with the Nez Percé was raging in Oregon at the time, and U.S. Army patrols under the command of General Oliver Howard roamed the area in search of "hostiles." One of General Howard's scouts came across what he believed was the grave of Mrs. Chambers and marked it well for future reference. Unable to return himself, years later he gave a prospector acquaintance named Duncan Teter directions to the gravesite. Teter reportedly found the grave but no gold.

But the legendary connection between the grave and the gold was not to be easily undone, and a perfectly believable explanation made the rounds among gold hunters. It was said that two Frenchmen had actually located the grave some years before and had discovered the gold. Deviously, they moved the headstone to another location to confuse the competition, but they were driven off by Indians before they could make the treasure theirs. The rich vein was surely still out there, marked by the woman's grave. Without a headstone, though, the grave would now be just that much harder to find.

After hearing the story of the Frenchmen, Teter reportedly went back into the wilderness and dug up the gravesite but found nothing except dirt. In the 1880s a Malheur County cattleman named B. Reaves developed an interest in the Blue Bucket Mine legend and spent a considerable amount of time looking for it. It was rumored that he found Chambers's grave with bones in it. But he found no gold, and some said it was the wrong grave. Eastern Oregon is a hard country, and many pioneers found their final resting place in a lonely corner of a meadow or forest. It would be easy enough to mistake the grave of another pioneer for Chambers's.

Then, in 1950, Mrs. Chambers's grave was reportedly found, headstone and all, by one Walter Meacham. The grave was located on a ranch in Agency Valley along the Little Malheur River. It is also believed to have been the same grave that B. Reaves claimed to have found.

But with the gravesite presumably known, where are the promised bucketfuls of gold? It's not so simple. How far does a wagon train pulled by oxen go in a day over mountain and forest terrain? And did the members of the wagon train travel one day or two days after burying Mrs. Chambers when they found the gold nuggets? Or was it before she died? And perhaps the knottiest piece of information to divine is what direction they were traveling. Most searchers have assumed the party was traveling west from the gravesite, toward the Willamette Valley, but some postulate that the terrain forced the party to travel south after burying Mrs. Chambers, which means that prospectors have been looking in entirely the wrong direction. Because so many accounts by the original Meek party members themselves vary, and are often contradictory, we will probably never know their exact route. Some doubt that the grave found in 1950 was really Chambers's. To date, the Lost Blue Bucket Mine remains lost.

The real question is this: Is a mother lode of gold really hidden along a small stream somewhere in the desert mountains of eastern Oregon, where desperately lost pioneers and serendipity briefly crossed paths in the wilderness more than a century and a half ago, or is it just another wild legend of the Wild West? And if the legend of the Lost Blue Bucket Mine is true, then how to find it? Calculated efforts over the decades have resulted in disappointment and even death. In the end, perhaps the Blue Bucket Mine, if it really exists, can only be found as its original discoverers did as their oxen-drawn wagons slowly inched toward the promised land: by accident, while seeking something far better than gold.

CHAPTER 6

THE HAUNTING OF HECETA HOUSE

In the depths of the night, with waves thundering against rocky shoreline, the coast of Oregon can sometimes be a lonely, and even spooky, place. The winter storms that regularly pound this rugged piece of North America can amplify those feelings as the fog blows in on a brisk wind and the roar of the sea overwhelms all other sounds. Sandwiched between the expanse of the Pacific Ocean and the dark, dense coniferous forest of the coastal mountains, it's the kind of place where the imagination can run free— or perhaps the intensity of this wild coast allows some people to see and experience things from the realm of the supernatural that are hidden to others. Heceta House and lighthouse may well be one of those places.

The concept of lighthouses to guide passing ships through treacherous waters dates back to the time of the ancient Greeks and Romans. During America's colonial period and in the early years of independence, the construction of lighthouses to guide ships of commerce was often championed by merchants and

U.S. FOREST SERVICE

Heceta House in the late 1800s or early 1900s.

other business interests who lobbied colonial governments or states to pick up the bill. But by the mid-1800s, as ship-based commerce came to America's West Coast, the federal government had assumed the role of providing for maritime safety, including building and operating the nation's lighthouses.

Nearly 165 ships sank in storms along the West Coast between 1849 and 1859, prompting the federal government to begin a program of lighthouse construction. It authorized funding for sixteen sites, although only one of those—the Umpqua River Lighthouse, which was built in 1857—was in Oregon.

Initially, most West Coast lighthouses were built off California, where the bulk of maritime commerce was taking place. But as business moved north, with goods being delivered or picked up by ships, the need arose for a system of lighthouses on the Oregon coast to warn seafarers away from its often-treacherous shore. There are currently nine lighthouses along Oregon's wild and stormy Pacific coast, constructed between the 1850s and the 1890s.

Heceta Head Lighthouse was one of those. It was built ostensibly to guide ships engaged in trading at Florence near the mouth of the Siuslaw River, but its main purpose was to light a dangerous "dark zone" along the coast between Cape Arago and Cape Foulweather. Congress appropriated $80,000 for the project in 1888. Constructed began in 1892 and was completed the following year. The finished facility consisted of a 56-foot-high lighthouse located on Heceta Head about 205 feet above the ocean, a house for the lightkeeper and his family, a duplex to house two assistant lightkeepers, and a barn and two sheds to store kerosene, all on 164 acres about 13 miles north of Florence that the federal government had purchased from homesteaders.

The original light was a five-wick kerosene lamp generating 80,000 candlepower that threw a beam twenty miles out to sea, thanks to a British-made eight-panel Fresnel lens. In 1934 the kerosene lamp was replaced with an electric bulb that boosted its power to one million candlepower and cast the light twenty-one miles out to sea. It was, and still is, the most powerful lighthouse on the Oregon coast.

Despite the area's raw beauty, Heceta Head was a lonely and remote posting for the men and families of the federal

Lighthouse Service, especially before the completion of the central Oregon coast section of the Roosevelt Coast Military Highway in 1932.

Although isolated from the many distractions of civilization, everyone had plenty to do. The wives occupied themselves with housekeeping and raising their children, while the men—lightkeeper and assistants—tended to the day-to-day lighthouse operations, which was no small chore.

Each day at sunset the lamp was lit, and then extinguished in the morning. The lenses that magnified the lamp's brightness revolved through a clockworks mechanism consisting of a system of hand-wound weights. As the gravity-driven weights slowly lowered through the bowels of the lighthouse, the lens turned. When the weights reached bottom, they were rewound, which had to be done every four hours. The light's timing was especially important. Heceta Head Lighthouse's lens revolved once every eight minutes and shot a burst of white light out to sea once per minute. This pattern identified Heceta Head so that ships passing in the night could pinpoint their position along the coast.

The work was divided among the three lightkeepers in shifts, with one shift lasting from sunset to midnight and the next from midnight to sunrise, an arrangement designed to allow each man to get a full night's sleep every three nights.

The first head keeper of Heceta Head Lighthouse was Andrew P. C. Hald. Not a great deal is known about the early keepers and their families, but suffice to say that the routine was generally the same for all of them, at least until Heceta Head was electrified and turned over to the U.S. Coast Guard for its operation between 1934 and 1939. In 1963 the lighthouse was fully automated. Soon after, the property and the lighthouse were procured by the State of Oregon, eventually coming under the management of the Oregon Department of Parks and Recreation with an agreement that the Coast Guard would maintain the property and facility in a "presentable condition." In 1965 the Coast Guard relinquished all of its responsibility for the lighthouse to the state.

During this time period, a series of caretakers moved into the assistants' house, known as Heceta House, under the employ of the state Parks and Recreation Department (the head light-keeper's house was torn down in 1940, and the wood was sold for another construction project). The first caretaker was Ken Lucas, who moved in with his family in 1963. Other caretakers followed in later years. In 1970 Lane Community College leased Heceta House for use in academic programs and took over the responsibility for hiring caretakers.

The life of the caretakers and their families was as routine as those of the original lightkeepers, although less rigorous and remote from civilization. They looked after the facilities, greeted visitors, and enjoyed life by the sea as they listened to the surf boom against the headland. It was a quiet and peaceful existence—until one night in November 1975.

Harry and Anne Tammen, the caretakers at the time, had come up from California in 1973 to live in Heceta House. While playing cards with a couple of friends on that November night, a high-pitched shriek suddenly pierced the night and echoed throughout the house. The color drained from the two couples' faces as they sat frozen in fear. It could only be Rue, the ghostly presence they already knew shared the house with them.

Soon after moving into Heceta House to begin their new jobs, the Tammens had started to wonder if there was more history to the old place than the legacy of the lighthouse and its hardy residents of times long past. They suspected, in fact, that perhaps one of them had never left.

For some time after arriving in their new home, the Tammens had been noting some strange, but subtle, goings-on. First there were the odd and eerie noises they initially dismissed as the creaking of old, warped floorboards, or the sea wind whistling down chimneys. Then things started to really get strange.

At one point, the couple thought the odd noises they heard from time to time might be emanating from the nocturnal activities of rodents or other furtive animals that might have invaded the house. To test that theory, one day they salted the attic with rat poison. When they went back to check to see if it had done its job, they found the poison gone and a silk stocking in its place. On other occasions, the Tammens would awaken in the morning to find open kitchen cupboard doors that they knew had been closed the previous night. Soon after the "card game scream," two community college students who were taking a study break by lounging on the front porch and enjoying the sea view were suddenly confronted with the chilling vision of a long, gray "it," as they described the experience, flowing up the porch steps like a wisp of smoke before it dissipated—or reached a destination hidden to their eyes.

The next appearance of the ghostly apparition of Heceta House came shortly after, and this time it revealed much more. The Tammens had hired several workmen to do some repairs on the house as well as a little painting. The men soon discovered it was not a typical job. Over the ensuing days they began to notice that tools went missing and that locked padlocks became inexplicably unlocked. At first they came up with logical explanations. They simply had misplaced the tools and needed to be more careful, or they forgot to snap the padlock completely closed and should double-check before they went home for the day. But as tools began disappearing and reappearing in the same locations, the men's previous explanations seemed less convincing. One of the workmen was soon to be presented with another very memorable explanation for these goings-on.

One day, workman Jim Anderson was up in the attic cleaning a window that faced the ocean when an odd reflection passed across the glass and he instinctively turned around. To his horror, staring back at him was an elderly woman with gray hair and dressed in a gown from the 1890s. As she regarded him with a wrinkled face that had seen many years of exposure to sun, wind, and salty air, Anderson could see that something was not quite right, and in a flash he scrambled through the attic trapdoor ladder and out of the house as fast as his legs would take him. For several days after, he flatly refused to return to Heceta House but eventually agreed to finish his work. Nothing, however, could convince him to venture back into the attic.

But the gray lady of Heceta House planned an encore. Anderson was working on the outside of the house when he accidentally broke one of the attic windows. Working from the exterior of the house, he replaced the glass but refused to go into the attic to sweep up the broken glass, which had fallen inside when the window was shattered. Late that night, the Tammens were roused from their sleep by the sounds of scraping and scratching coming from the attic overhead. Although they were not aware that the workman had broken the window, the couple commented that it sounded like someone sweeping glass. The next morning, they went into the attic to investigate and found the broken glass, neatly swept into a pile. The Tammens made the mistake of telling the story to the workmen when they arrived that day, and the crew left the job site, this time for good.

As would be expected, there was a great deal of discussion and speculation about who the mysterious apparition might be. Eventually two stories emerged. According to the first, and most accepted, version, the gray lady of Heceta House is the wife of one of the first lightkeepers, whose child died and was buried on the premises. Now she wanders the house (and the grounds as well) in search of her long-lost child and is reluctant to leave her home by the sea. Her name, Rue, was identified during a Ouija

board session, although when it took place and who participated in the ritual were not recorded. The daughter of Olaf L.
Hansen, who was Heceta Head's chief lightkeeper from 1904
to 1920, reported that located between Heceta House and the
lighthouse was a small cement slab, which was believed to be
the headstone of a baby girl's grave. The grave has long since
become overgrown, and its location is lost. Perhaps it is this
child for which Rue mourns? Another, less popular telling of
the story has it that the ghost is of the baby girl herself in search
of her mother.

The Tammens reported seeing Rue several times as they
went about their caretaking duties, and over the years she continued to make her presence known to the various residents of
Heceta House. Some even claimed to have seen Rue in her wispy
smoke form gliding along the beach.

In the early 1990s Duncan and Carolyn Stockton took
over as caretakers and soon were introduced to the house's
"other" resident. This took the form of strange noises outside
their bedroom door late at night, or the sound of someone
unseen coming up the gravel pathway to the house. Just like
the workmen of the 1970s, Duncan Stockton also had tools go
missing. Once, he even got a look at the gray lady through the
north-facing attic window.

Today, in addition to being a national historic site managed by the Oregon Department of Parks and Recreation, Heceta House is operated as a bed-and-breakfast, and Rue has taken

the opportunity to introduce herself to the house's guests along with its caretakers.

Those guests have their own ghost stories to tell. In one instance, a couple staying at the house for their twenty-fifth wedding anniversary had an eerie encounter in the wee morning hours. At about 4:00 a.m. the woman awoke to the sound of a strange buzzing sound that engulfed her head. Too afraid to look, she nevertheless could detect a bright light through her tightly shut eyelids as she felt something touch her hand. Startled, she opened her eyes, only to behold an orb of red light pass right through the closed bedroom door. The next morning, thinking that the experience was far too bizarre to be anything more than a dream, she let it pass out of her thoughts—that is, until her husband asked her if she had noticed the weird glowing light that he saw hovering over their bed early that morning before dawn.

An alleged guest encounter with Rue that is considered to be one of the more credible sightings happened in 2001 when two professional photographers were staying at the house while working on a photo essay. While photographing outside the house one day, they looked up to see someone through the window in one of the photographers' rooms. Later that day when the photographer mentioned the incident to the innkeeper, he was told that nobody was in the house at the time he saw the figure in the window. Upset at this revelation, he looked around in his room, discovering that a few of his things had disappeared, as things tend to do every now and then at Heceta House.

Mysteriously locked doors are another recurring event at Heceta House, and caretakers tell of bathroom doors secured with deadbolts that can only be locked from inside—but no one is in the bathroom.

Another guest was abruptly roused from his slumber by the sound of loud banging that he initially thought might be coming from the house's old water pipes. Then the room became very warm, a phenomenon commonly associated with the ghostly manifestations at Heceta House. One of the more amusing stories told by a guest was of a door that opened by itself—and let the resident cat out.

In a 2002 encounter a hiker and her dog one winter night walked up the trail from the parking lot, past Heceta House to the lighthouse, her flashlight illuminating the way. As they approached the lighthouse, the woman's canine companion began to shake in fear and refused to approach any closer. Squinting in the darkness, she suddenly spotted a figure wrapped in a cloak standing at the edge of the headland, looking out toward the dark ocean. The hiker's first instinct was to walk over and say hello to the lonely watcher, but her dog, now verging on near panic, convinced her otherwise, and both turned and made double-time back to her car.

While encounters with Rue or experiencing some of her manifestations may be terrifying for some, the caretakers who spent time living with her in Heceta House all tell the same story—that she means no ill will toward the living and seems most concerned that "her" home is well cared for. In fact, care-takers have often reported that she usually makes her presence known when someone has tried to make modifications to the house, has made a mess, or is just being a sloppy housekeeper. In such cases she may show up with her broom or remove something carelessly left lying about by the living.

Although one of the better-known hauntings in Oregon, Rue and Heceta House received national fame in 2000 when her story was told as part of a History Channel special on ghost stories of the Pacific Northwest.

Many things have changed since the kerosene light first flickered on at Heceta Head Lighthouse in 1893. Roads have been built, and the lightkeepers who toiled each night year-round to help guide ships past perilous shores are long gone, replaced by electricity and automation. What was once an important facility manned by proud employees of the federal Lighthouse Service with a serious job to do is now a popular visitor attraction, where you can take guided tours of the lighthouse and Heceta House, and even stay the night if it suits your fancy.

But other things remain the same. Heceta Head Lighthouse still casts its lifesaving beam out to sea as the surf booms against the headland and the dense fog drifts in to engulf the dark forest. And if the many lightkeepers and their families have gone on to become part of this place's history, one still apparently remains in her beloved home on this wild, Oregon coastal headland: Rue, the gray lady of Heceta House.

CHAPTER 7

THE WRECK OF THE BEESWAX GALLEON

The year was 1707, and the Spanish galleon *San Francisco Xavier* out of Manila, Philippines, was hopelessly overdue at the Spanish colonial port of Acapulco on the Pacific coast of Mexico. There its cargo of riches from Asia was to be off-loaded, carried overland to Veracruz, and then shipped across the Atlantic Ocean to Spain. Although impressive in size and majestic under full sail, the galleons were always at risk on their transpacific voyages. Known as the Manila Galleons, they were heavily loaded down with passengers and valuable cargo; as such, they were low-riding, slow-moving ships that were very vulnerable to pirates and storms. Often, when a galleon failed to arrive at its appointed destination, its fate and the location of its demise could be determined by wreckage drifting ashore in the wake of a typhoon, or from loose talk at seaports frequented by pirates and other nefarious characters who roamed the seas. In other cases, such as that of the *San Francisco Xavier,* galleons simply vanished without a trace. In those days there was no way to launch a search for missing vessels, and authorities and family members of the ships' passengers and crew simply accepted the fact that the sea had swallowed them forever and that their ultimate resting place would never be discovered.

Of the six Manila Galleons known to have vanished at sea somewhere between the Philippines and Mexico between 1578 and 1750, one may have come to its end on the Oregon coast, and some believe that galleon was the *San Francisco Xavier*. If it was the *San Francisco Xavier,* or even another Manila galleon, it not only would solve the mystery of the ship's disappearance but also would represent the first recorded contact of Europeans with Pacific Northwest native tribes. Clues to this centuries-old mystery include a "red-haired" Indian who visited the Lewis and Clark expedition at their winter quarters on the lower Columbia River in 1805; tons of beeswax blocks with strange markings gathered up from the beach by the Indians, and later by white settlers; and tales of the battered hulk of an old sailing ship made of teakwood in the manner of a Spanish galleon found near the mouth of the Nehalem River, thirty miles south of the mouth of the Columbia River, and now long since buried by the shifting sands. These clues and others have sparked a search for the "beeswax galleon" and its treasures that has lasted for more than a hundred years.

The year 1492 was a precipitous one in world history, and even more so for Spain. In that year, Spain became a nation unto itself after finally driving the last of the occupying Muslim Moors

Frank J. Kumm, custodian of the Pioneer Museum of Tillamook,
Oregon, holds beeswax from Nehalem Peninsula, 1952.

from the Iberian Peninsula, a process that took nearly eight hundred years. That same year, Christopher Columbus, sailing under the Spanish flag in search of a direct water route to Asia, made landfall on a small Caribbean island off the coast of North America and "discovered" a new world of which Europeans had no previous knowledge. That accidental discovery, along with another by a Spanish explorer twenty-nine years later, would be instrumental in making Spain for a time a world superpower and the richest country in Europe. It would also set a beeswax galleon on a collision course with the Oregon coast.

Although Columbus's quest to reach the East Indies trade markets by sea had failed, the Spanish nevertheless wasted little time in exploring their newly claimed territory to see what riches it might yield, for this emerging nation needed money to fund its designs for empire abroad and to pay for wars against its enemies at home. The New World would not disappoint.

In 1519 eleven ships carrying six hundred Spanish conquistadores under the command of Hernán Cortés landed on the east coast of Mexico. Marching on Tenochtitlán, capital of the fabulously wealthy Aztec empire, Cortés alternately negotiated for peace and attacked. Finally, in 1521, Cortés and his men, aided by thousands of Indian allies fed up with Aztec rule, took Tenochtitlán and subdued the Aztecs' central Mexican empire. A dozen years later, another conquistador named Francisco Pizarro conquered the equally rich Inca empire in Peru. This vast New World wealth—gold, silver, emeralds, jade, textiles, and more—started being shipped in a regular stream of "treasure fleets" to Spain for deposit in the royal treasury.

In April 1521, another Spanish adventurer, Ferdinand Magellan, was putting ashore on an island in what is today the Philippines to replenish supplies of food and water. Commanding five ships, he was trying to find the all-water trade route to the Far East that Columbus had failed to locate. Unfortunately for Magellan, the indigenous people weren't friendly, and they attacked when he and his men landed on the beach. Magellan was among the casualties. His crew, under his second-in-command Juan Sebastian Elcano, sailed off. They eventually returned to Spain in the one surviving ship, circumnavigating the globe in the process.

Magellan's accidental discovery of the Philippines was an extremely fortuitous circumstance, for the archipelago was perfectly situated as a staging area for trade with East Indian and Asian markets. And now it was on Spanish charts. The Spanish returned and by 1565 had begun to colonize the island chain. In 1571 they established the city of Manila on the island of Luzon.

Now, with a base in the Pacific, where goods could be transferred to their own ships for transport, Spain was in a favorable position to exploit the spice trade. There was only one problem. The Portuguese controlled the Indian Ocean, and later the Dutch controlled the waters off the Cape of Good Hope and would not allow the passage of enemy ships through their territory. For the Spanish, that meant that an all-water route by India and around Africa was not available to them.

However, because Spain also controlled Mexico, which they christened New Spain, it had a viable alternative. Goods from the Asian and East Indian markets could be shipped by sea to the port of Acapulco on Mexico's west coast, carried overland to Veracruz (established by Cortés when he first arrived in Mexico) on the east coast, and then shipped across the Atlantic Ocean to Spain. In this way, trade goods and commerce constantly flowed between Manila, New Spain, and the Spanish homeland. The vessels that carried these goods on the Pacific Ocean leg were the famed Manila Galleons.

Galleons, a standard class of ship used by European nations from the 1500s into the 1700s, served as both warships and commercial vessels. Typically weighing less than five hundred tons, with high poop decks, and broad of beam, they were powered by three to five sails. Because the Manila Galleons were intended to carry cargo, they were much larger than the typical galleon. Some were more than 160 feet long and displaced two thousand tons of water. Most of them were constructed in the Philippines of indigenous hardwoods such as teak.

The voyage from Manila to Acapulco took about four months. Because prevailing wind patterns were less favorable for ships traveling west, the trip from Acapulco to Manila lasted a couple of months longer.

In the galleons' holds were silk, porcelain, fine china, ivory, a variety of spices, and beeswax from Asian bees, a valuable commodity in New Spain for the manufacture of candles since no honeybees were native to the Americas. These goods from the Asian and Spice Island markets were paid for with silver from Mexico.

Because the Manila–Acapulco trade was a crown monopoly, government administrators closely regulated it. Cargo space on each galleon was carefully measured in sections (called *piezas*) that were two and one-fifth feet long, two feet wide, and ten inches deep. Each galleon had about four thousand *piezas,* which were allotted to merchants, government agents, and pensioners. The galleons also carried passengers, usually persons of importance on royal or other business.

For all their visual majesty, a transoceanic crossing on a Manila galleon was not especially pleasant. In addition to all the merchandise, the holds and decks were stuffed with barrels of food and water and other supplies for the four- to six-month journey. Provisions included a regular menagerie of animals, such as chickens and swine, to provide a source of fresh meat. Dried water buffalo meat was a staple, and water was doled out in small doses, because on the open sea it is a ship's most valuable commodity. Rats thrived in this filthy environment, and a variety of diseases could run rampant as well, making sickness a regular part of a voyage on a Manila galleon. Despite these hardships, in their nearly three-hundred-year history some 110 Manila galleons sailed between Manila and Acapulco.

At first three ships sailed each year, but because of the hazards of the journey, including storms and pirates, Spanish

Aerial view of Nehalem Bay at the mouth of the Nehalem River, where the beeswax galleon is believed to have run aground.

merchants had a law passed in 1593 limiting them to two departures per year to reduce their potential losses.

The first inkling that one of those long-ago losses may have washed up on the shores of Oregon came on December 31, 1805, when a group of Clatsop Indians dropped by the winter quarters of the Lewis and Clark expedition near the present-day city of Astoria on Oregon's north coast. Clark noted in his journal that one of the natives was a man in his mid-twenties with long red hair and freckles and "certainly must be half white at least." Clark also commented that the man understood more English than the others in his band but exhibited Indian customs in every other way.

In 1811, a year after Fort Astoria was established by John Jacob Astor's fur trading company, one of his men, Gabriel

Franchere, visited a Native American village while traveling up the Columbia River on an exploratory mission. At the village, he met an elderly man named Soto. With the aid of an interpreter, Soto explained that he was the son of a Spanish sailor, a crew member of a ship that had been wrecked in a storm at the river's mouth. Soto related that a large number of the sailors survived the storm and managed to get to shore safely, but the Indians soon set upon them and killed all but four. The surviving members of the crew, which included his father, were taken in by the Indians and eventually married Native American wives. Over time, however, the Spaniards tired of the wild life the Indians led and set out through the wilderness in search of a settlement populated by Europeans, leaving their offspring behind. The four were never seen or heard from again, and their fate remains unknown to this day.

A couple of years later, Alexander Henry, a fur trader and trapper with the British-owned Northwest Company, recorded in his journal on December 8, 1813, an encounter he had with an "old Clatsop chief" at the mouth of the Columbia River. Accompanying the chief was a man about thirty-five years old with very dark red hair; supposedly he was the son of a sailor who had been shipwrecked on the coast many years earlier. A year later, another visitor to Astoria mentioned meeting an Indian man from a coastal tribe to the south of the Columbia River. Unlike his fellow tribal members, he was tall and slender and most notably was fair-skinned and freckled, with bright red hair. His name was Jack Ramsey, and he said he was the son of an English seaman who had deserted his ship years earlier and had lived among the Indians for some time. The father had died some twenty years before and had sired a number of offspring, although Jack was the only red-haired one of the lot.

These tales were extremely intriguing to early white visitors to the north Oregon coast, and their similarities strongly suggested that a Spanish ship had wrecked somewhere in the area many years earlier. Although the story of the "white" Indian with a ship-jumping English father seems to throw a monkey wrench in the theory, that is not necessarily the case. Because genes for dark hair are dominant, he would have had to inherit his red hair from both parents. That is entirely plausible, as the native woman his English father married could very easily have been a descendant of one of the shipwrecked Spaniards; as such, she could have carried her ancestors' predisposition for red hair.

The story of a Spanish shipwreck firmly ensconced itself in the oral traditions of local tribes. Settler Silas Smith—whose father was a trapper who had settled in Oregon in 1823 and had married the daughter of Cob-a-Way, the chief of the Clatsop tribe—related how his mother's people told a story of a large ship that came aground at the mouth of the Nehalem River. According to this story, virtually all the sailors survived and lived peacefully for a time among the tribe. But eventually, the whites began to run into trouble, especially involving disrespect for the Indians' marital traditions, and the Indians killed them.

A white man named Warren Vaughn, who spent the years 1852–1853 visiting the Nehalem area, told another version of the beeswax galleon story. He said that all of the crew were killed by Indians, except for a black man who integrated into the Nehalem tribe, married one of its women, and had a number of children. After speaking with various tribal members and determining that none of them were telling the story from personal recollection but rather were passing down a tribal legend, he estimated that the shipwreck occurred sometime between 1690 and 1740.

Vaughn also heard another story about a second ship that landed on the coast near Neahkahnie Mountain, just north of Nehalem Bay. From that ship five or six men rowed a small boat ashore and buried a chest somewhere on the mountain. Then they placed a large boulder to mark the spot. But before leaving, they killed one of their number and laid him astride the boulder so that his spirit would protect the chest's contents or perhaps simply to scare away curious interlopers. Vaughn heard this story from a very elderly and nearly blind woman of the tribe who claimed she had witnessed this incident when she was a small girl while picking berries on Neahkahnie Mountain.

Before long, the story of a ship whose crew buried treasure on Neahkahnie Mountain sometimes became intertwined with the tale of the beeswax galleon. One such story came from Silas Smith's aunt, Mrs. Edward Gervais, who was also Chief Cob-a-Way's daughter. In the version she heard in her youth, the Spanish ship crashed onto the shore during a nighttime storm, and about thirty of the crew survived. The tribe was amazed at the cornucopia of never-before-seen goods and objects floating in the waves and carried up onto the beach. In her version, it was the crew of the broken galleon who buried the chest and its unknown contents on Neahkahnie Mountain and placed a rock to mark its resting place.

This version of the beeswax galleon story inevitably spurred rumors of lost pirate treasure buried on the coastal peak, and many people scoured its forested flanks in a fruitless search for the buried chest. In 1890 a treasure hunter discovered a stone carved with letters, numbers, and other symbols on the lower slopes of the mountain. More similarly marked stones were found in the same area years later, but their purpose and meaning were never ascertained. Treasure hunters were still looking well into the mid-twentieth century, with no success.

Perhaps the most interesting version of how the beeswax galleon came to its final resting place on the Oregon shore was passed on by a longtime resident of the area who heard it from the Nehalem Indians when he was a boy. According to this story, early one morning two ships appeared on the horizon, with one chasing the other. The Nehalem Indians watched from shore in tense fascination as bursts of smoke and the sound of thunder emanated from each ship. Although they had no idea what was happening, they were witnessing a furious sea battle that lasted throughout the day. Being pursued, the larger ship ran aground near the mouth of the Nehalem River during the course of the battle and stuck fast. But at nightfall the attacking ship's captain apparently decided he could not take his quarry, and the ship snuck away under cover of darkness. The sixty or so survivors of the stranded ship rowed ashore with a large chest that they buried on the slopes of Neahkahnie Mountain and piled stones over where it was buried. Then they built cabins along the shoreline and established a small settlement. They lived peacefully for a few years but then began to insult and attack the Nehalem women. In revenge the tribe's warriors killed the white interlopers.

This story clearly combines a number of the traditional story lines of the beeswax galleon wreck. Although most researchers dismiss the idea of buried treasure associated with the galleon, a battle with another ship is not beyond the realm of possibility. Manila Galleons were a favorite quarry of pirates. A ship might have been driven aground while trying to escape buccaneers, thus explaining how a Manila galleon came to be so far north of the standard ocean route to Acapulco.

Just as intriguing as the stories and legends was fur trader Alexander Henry's observation that the Indians, whose number included the red-haired man, often traded large pieces of beeswax that they dug up from the sand on the beach south of Astoria on the Nehalem River spit. Here, they said, is where the Spanish ship went aground many years ago and most of the crew were massacred. The chunks of beeswax were part of its surviving cargo, scattered across the sandy spit in large numbers and still easily salvaged.

Beeswax was known to be a common cargo item on the Manila Galleons. It was gathered from Asian bees in Cambodia and Siam (now Thailand) to satisfy Spain's huge demand for millions of candles for lighting homes, illuminating church altars, and other uses. Because native North American bees do not produce wax, the wax the Indians brought in to trade could not have come from an indigenous source.

For the local natives, this beeswax-laden beach was their equivalent of a gold mine. By the 1840s the Hudson Bay Company had established itself in the Oregon country for the purpose of trading in local goods such as fur and salmon. When the Indians discovered that the traders were also interested in beeswax, they began making regular trips to the beach at the mouth of the Nehalem River to excavate the strange but valuable material.

The pieces they brought in for trade ranged in size from small round chunks to blocks weighing as much as seventy-five pounds. The larger pieces were approximately the size of *piezas,* adding to the speculation that years earlier they had spilled from the cargo hold of a Manila galleon.

Some of the bigger pieces were stamped with large letters, numbers, or symbols, causing curiosity among natives and whites alike as to their meaning and origin. Later, as the nineteenth century wore on and whites established permanent settlements along the Oregon coast, they, too, set out to gather beeswax on the beaches where the Nehalem River meets the sea, adding to the collection of marked specimens.

As more and more pieces were mined from the sands, these markings became the subject of considerable speculation over the years. The symbols and patterns included a large *N* with a diamond pattern cut above it, as well as *IHN* and *IHS*, which some thought stood for *In Hoc Nomen* (in his name) and *In Hoc Signo* (in his sign), respectively. Others surmised that the latter meant *Jesus Hominum Salvator*. But this was little more than guesswork, and the most likely explanation was that these symbols were trademarks of some kind, perhaps denoting ownership of the beeswax bars.

One piece of beeswax, now residing in the Tillamook County Pioneer Museum, has the numbers *67* and *1679* inscribed on it, the latter supposedly indicating a year. In 1961 this piece of beeswax was dated via carbon-14 testing and was estimated to have been about 280 years old at the time, meaning that it originated in the 1680s. Further microscopic study of the sample found bee stingers and plant pollen native to Southeast Asia. Radiocarbon dating performed in the 1980s found that the beeswax was produced between 1430 and 1830.

Popular accounts suggest that as much as four hundred tons of beeswax were recovered from the sands of the Nehalem beach. However, in 1909 a University of Oregon researcher conducted a study by looking at historical trade records and estimated the figure to be closer to twelve tons.

The sheer amount of beeswax, along with its estimated age, provides strong proof that its source was a Manila galleon.

But even more proof emerged in the 1840s in the form of the remains of the galleon itself.

The first report of the wreckage, in 1844, placed it about forty miles south of the Columbia River near the mouth of the Nehalem, just as the old stories had described. The wreck was reported by others on and off into the late 1890s. Some claimed seeing two different wrecks near the river's mouth; these reports suggest that the galleon may have broken in two when it washed ashore. Since the turn of the twentieth century, the mystery ship's remains have alternately appeared and disappeared with the blowing winds and shifting sands. Those who had the opportunity to examine it say it was made of teakwood, a typical construction material for a Manila galleon.

One of the last times it was seen was in 1929, when British vice consul at Astoria, E. M. Cherry, who apparently subscribed to the treasure chest version of the galleon story, planned to raise the hull from the sand and muck to claim the valuables he believed it held. However, the project's estimated $30,000 cost was more than he could afford, and his plan fizzled.

Other clues have been found as well, including pieces of ceramics that date from the same time period as the beeswax, and some Chinese coins that for a time spawned a now discredited theory that the wreck was a Chinese or Japanese junk.

So much evidence argues for a Manila galleon that historians have combed the records of the ships' voyages between Manila and Acapulco, focusing on ships that were lost at sea for reasons unknown. Of the six that fit that category, two disappeared well before the estimated age of the Nehalem beeswax, and the fates of three others have since been tentatively ascertained.

That leaves the *San Francisco Xavier,* under the command of Santiago Zabalburú, which sailed from Manila in January 1707 with two hundred people on board, never to be seen again. It was loaded with about $4 million worth of cargo, including silk, gold ingots, porcelain, spices, and as much as eighty-seven tons of beeswax. It never reached Acapulco and may very well be the mystery beeswax galleon. It might have been driven far off course by a violent storm that pitched the great ship onto the beach on the Oregon coast, breaking it in two, and most of its crew might have been killed by the local natives, leaving a legacy of Indian legends, pioneer stories, and a beach scattered with beeswax.

Perhaps the only sure way to solve the mystery of the beeswax galleon is to find its surviving hulk, which has not been seen in many decades. The search goes on, most recently by a coalition of scientists who have formed a group called the Beeswax Shipwreck Project. They have been searching for the wreck using modern scientific instruments, although so far to no avail. Yet maybe one day the fickle winds of the Pacific Ocean will begin to blow at just the right speed and in the just the right direction, scouring away the sand at just the right spot. And then the beeswax galleon, lost for so many centuries, will rise to the surface again to finally reveal its identity and tell us its story.

CHAPTER 8

THE OREGON VORTEX

There are a few places on planet Earth that defy the immutable laws of physics, where gravity no longer functions properly and things do not appear as our senses and instincts tell us they should. One of the most famous of these mysterious phenomena can be found in the small historic town of Gold Hill, just off Interstate 5 in the southwestern part of the state at a place known as the Oregon Vortex.

To physicists, a vortex is a spirally spinning flow of air or liquid with a central core that can produce a great deal of turbulent energy, with "vortex lines" radiating out from that core. Dust devils and tornadoes are examples of vortexes. But the Oregon Vortex is a strange and powerful energy field that is capable of rendering the laws of nature moot.

Located about ten miles east of Grants Pass in Jackson County, Gold Hill was the site of one of the earliest gold discoveries in southwestern Oregon, from which it derived its name. A U.S. post office was officially established there in 1884, and eleven years later the town was incorporated, populated mostly by gold miners in search of their fortunes.

Today, Gold Hill residents are proud of their city (population: about 1,100) and its historic past, evident in much of the town's old-time architecture. In 1986 the community formed the Gold Hill Historical Society and set up headquarters in the Beeman-Martin House, built in 1901 with money made, appropriately enough, from the Lucky Bart Mine.

Before the miners came, the local Indian tribes also knew about Gold Hill—not for its yellow ore, for which they had no use, but for its strange and unnatural properties. This small area, which the Indians reportedly referred to as "the forbidden ground," lay across the Rogue River from where gold was first discovered. Wild animals gave the spot a wide berth, and the Indians avoided it as well.

Early settlers to Gold Hill were aware of Native American stories about this curious circular area, which they estimated to be about three-quarters of an acre: People's height changed from spot to spot, they had to lean toward magnetic north regardless of the slope of the land on which they stood, and objects rolled uphill, among other strange goings-on.

But the business of the original residents of Gold Hill was getting rich, not investigating the mysteries of the universe, so the oddity of the place remained just that. In fact, the Grey Eagle Mining Company in the 1890s constructed a gold assay office on the mystery spot, where the quality, and therefore value, of

Mildred and John Litster at the entrance of the Oregon Vortex, at Sardine Creek near Gold Hill, fall 1954. Oregon Vortex manager Fred Coffman is at the far right.

miners' gold was determined. For a time, the office's location at the center of what would eventually be identified as a vortex did not seem to have any ill effects on business or otherwise—until 1910, when a heavy rainstorm caused the building to come off its foundation and slide downhill, ending up against a large maple tree, where it rests to this day, no longer level but otherwise largely unscathed.

A few years after the assay office's wild ride on a mudslide, John Litster heard about some of the strange and unnatural phenomena that reportedly occurred on the site. He visited

Gold Hill hoping to put those stories to the rigors of scientific experimentation.

Born in Alva, Scotland, in 1886 and the son of a British foreign diplomat, John Litster was a physicist, mining engineer, and geologist who eventually moved to Gold Hill. In 1913 he reportedly conducted fourteen thousand individual experiments to discern the nature and causes of the anomalies on that mysterious three-quarter-acre plot.

Strange phenomena reported by those who dared to enter the mysterious circle had so far confounded normal, rational explanations. The oddities were wide-ranging and included brooms that stood on end, people and sticks growing or shrinking depending on their location, balls rolling uphill, people unable to stand straight against a plumb line, and feelings of nausea and disorientation as if struggling to stand on the deck of a ship riding stormy seas.

Litster's experiments led him to conclude that Gold Hill—at coordinates 42°29'40" N and 123°5' W—sat amid an electromagnetic antigravitational vortex, 165.375 feet in circumference and surrounded by a corona extending 27.5625 feet outside the vortex proper, for a total affected area of 220.5 feet. He was able to calculate the existence of the corona with a magnet. When he placed an object or a person on the vortex's line of demarcation, the subjects exhibited the characteristic leaning stance. He then moved the magnet inward toward the vortex sphere until the subjects stood erect. This occurred at the 27.5625-foot position. In addition, the area also exhibited a number of smaller, satellite vortexes with similar properties. Intersecting the principal vortex are a number of "Terralines" arranged in both east-west and north-south configurations. He determined that each line was fifty-seven inches wide and, within those lines, exhibits some of the same strange powers as the central Gold Hill vortex. He further concluded that the Terralines oscillated where they crossed through the vortex, offsetting the line between where it entered and where it exited.

He counted a total of fifteen Terralines, eleven of which entered the Gold Hill vortex and four that brush its edges. Oscillation periods take place in 22.33-second blocks, remaining stationary for a little more than eleven seconds. According to Litster's surviving scientific notes, "when the North line moves West, the South line moves East; when the North line moves east, then the South line moves West." Then the movements reverse. He declared these movements to be "concerted and continuous" and concluded that it was an example of reverse oscillation. As for the Terralines outside of the vortex sphere, he found that although they did not exhibit any oscillation, they did move a total of 14.25 inches in concert with the Terralines within or in contact with the vortex.

Litster also concluded that the vortex changed periodically in size over the course of each day, expanding by 19 inches at sunrise; contracting by 19 inches in late morning, at noon, and in the afternoon; and then contracting by a whopping 361 inches at sunset.

He noted that lead shields do not affect the penetrating power of the vortex, a Geiger counter detects no radioactivity in the area, and photographic techniques used to record radiation turned up negative. Magnetic compasses used on the Terralines he found were also not affected. Litster claimed that, curiously, gold in some instances was capable of absorbing the vortex's energy waves. Trees growing on or near the Terralines bent their branches toward them and along their lines.

Taking his investigations further afield, he extrapolated his data beyond the immediate vicinity to encompass the surrounding region. According to Litster, after checking approximately thirty thousand square miles, Terralines were documented extending through the Siskiyou summit, about forty-five miles southwest of the vortex. He also claimed to have found additional Terralines, with varying electromagnetic properties, extending from Grants Pass west to the Pacific Ocean and south to Monterey Bay in California. His research in this area indicated that there were Terralines along a fifty- to eighty-mile-wide corridor along the West Coast from approximately Gold Beach to Monterey. He also calculated that as of 1953 he had identified at least seven other vortexes with properties similar to the Gold Hill vortex within the United States, with the nearest located on the summit of the Siskiyou mountain range. Litster also speculated that the Terralines he had mapped, rather than being localized to the Pacific coast, might in fact be a global phenomenon, so he recommended further future study.

In addition to his experiments divining the electromagnetic properties of the place, he also conducted a number of empirical experiments and demonstrations that exemplified the unusual properties of the vortex. One such demonstration involves a subject standing within the vortex, straight as an arrow, with a plumb line dangling from his belt, and his posture aligned with the plumb line. But when the subject is directed to stand with his left foot on ground through which a Terraline passes, he leans notably toward magnetic north, clearly "off plumb."

In another experiment, two men of similar height stand opposite each other on an inclining plank. In this situation, the man on the left appears taller than the man on the right. When they switch places, the man who in the first situation appeared taller now appears shorter, with the other man exhibiting the opposite effect. According to Litster's documentation, the maximum effect occurs when the two subjects are placed in close alignment at a position of 23°27' from true north and south.

This apparent change in the height of people and objects is a primary and most commonly observed property of the Oregon Vortex, and Litster spent a considerable amount of time and effort to explain it. His explanation focused on the presence of atoms that existed within the vortex's field. Because the vortex's axis is inclined in a north-south direction as well as warped, any atoms along these axes also exhibit a corresponding aberration that results in physical changes of any objects (including human beings) found within the vortex field. Light refracted within the vortex sphere contributed to the apparent change of height, even when one of the subjects remained outside the vortex and the other stood within it. Litster claimed that the height distortion and other phenomena exhibited within the vortex could also be observed outside the vortex, as long as one stood on a Terraline.

Unfortunately, only a smattering of the Scottish engineer's notes and documentary photographs survive. Upon completing his experiments, he reportedly destroyed most of his writings on the subject, feeling that his findings were so contrary to what people have come to believe is natural that the world was not prepared for what he had learned about this mysterious and sometimes feared place. He was purported to have said, as he burned his papers, "The world is not ready for this."

However, eventually Litster must have had a change of heart, because by the 1920s he had acquired the old Grey Eagle Mine site, including the vortex, publicized the discovery of its anomalies, and opened it as a tourist attraction around 1930. It was known as "The Fabulous Oregon Vortex and the House of Mystery"—the latter being the old assay building, where the powers of the vortex are at their apex.

Litster died in 1959, having spent decades running the attraction and working to prove his "Theory of Mass Change," which postulates that when people walk along electromagnetic Terralines, their bodies actually condense or expand. He believed that his theory could be demonstrated at the vortex. It is said that Litster even consulted with Albert Einstein on the subject. A couple of years after Litster's death, a local Gold Hill family, the Coopers, bought the twenty-two-acre property from his widow and continued to operate it as a roadside attraction. Over the decades, the Oregon Vortex and House of Mystery has become easily the most famous paranormal site in the United States and has inspired many imitators.

There are at least twenty-eight other claimed vortex sites in the United States and another in Canada. In 1941 Litster acted as a consultant for the Mystery Spot in Santa Cruz, California, helping to determine the best locations to demonstrate that vortex's powers. In the 1950s he likely also helped set up the Cosmos of the Black Hills in South Dakota, another vortex-based roadside attraction.

The focus of a visit to the Oregon Vortex includes the House of Mystery and a couple of demonstration locations to show off the site's unusual properties. One such demonstration involves two poles, both seven feet tall, placed on opposite ends of a plank on a north-south line. Yet the pole on the north end seems to be a few inches shorter than the other pole. The phenomenon applies equally to people. If two people start on each end and walk toward and past each other on the plank, they will seem to change height, either shorter or taller depending on whether they are moving to the north or the south.

For another demonstration, a visitor stands at the center of the plank while someone else stands to the north, and both appear to be the same height. But when one person edges over to the south side of the plank, he or she mysteriously becomes much taller than the other, and the first person has to reach up to touch the other's shoulder.

A different experience altogether awaits in the topsy-turvy House of Mystery, where visitors involuntarily lean off center and some even get a little seasick as if magnetic powers are creeping inside their bodies. Other, equally disconcerting experiences inside the former assay office include a ball that seems to roll uphill, a platform where visitors instinctively lean as much as 7 degrees toward magnetic north, a broom that stands upright, and a pendulum that swings farther in one direction than the other.

After an excursion to the Oregon Vortex, many visitors come away believers, but skeptics say it is all optical illusions and no more than that.

Despite its claimed electromagnetic powers, some believe that the Oregon Vortex is an example of a broader category of phenomena known as "gravity hills" or "magnetic hills." In these places, the terrain and visual reference points create optical illusions that make uphill appear to be downhill. Thus, vehicles and balls may seem to roll uphill. The lack of a clear horizon to use as a reference point is often a crucial factor in making the illusion seem real, since estimating the direction of a slope— especially a gradual slope—can be problematic without such a reference point.

While this might seem to be an unusual circumstance, gravity hills, and the combination of terrain that creates them, are fairly common throughout the world, and at least forty-nine have been identified in the United States—including the Oregon Vortex. Generally, these areas have a hilly or rolling terrain, and a level horizon is not readily visible.

The semicircular canals within the inner ear help humans keep their balance and determine which way is up and which way is down. One canal can detect horizontal movements of the head, and two canals positioned at 45-degree angles keep tabs on vertical head movements. With head movements, fluid within those canals sloshes back and forth, sending the appropriate information to the brain.

While this is a very efficient system for maintaining balance and orientation, people also rely on visual cues for this information. If those cues are muddled or absent, they can overpower our perception of visual reality, making things appear larger or smaller than they really are and making vertical objects seem off-kilter. It can even be difficult to check for such optical illusions because without a good horizon as a visual checkpoint, a plumb line may appear to confirm the illusion.

Pertinent to this type of mind trick is what is known as the Ponzo illusion, named after the Italian psychologist Mario Ponzo, who demonstrated it in 1913—coincidentally the same year Litster began his research on the Oregon Vortex. The idea is that humans gauge the size of an object based on its background. For example, converging lines can make a distant object look longer or larger than a close object, even though they are the same size. In another example, a full moon may look unnaturally large because buildings, trees, and other objects in the foreground fool our sense of perspective.

No matter whether the phenomenon is an optical illusion or a mysterious force, electromagnetic or otherwise, believers and skeptics alike still flock to the Oregon Vortex and the House of Mystery every year. Already a well-known attraction, the vortex became even more famous when it was mentioned in the December 15, 1999, episode of *The X-Files*.

But the questions remain. Is it real? Do strange powers accumulate in that 165-foot-plus sphere, which condenses body mass, shifts the sizes of objects, and causes people to surrender to the irresistible urge to lean into magnetic north? There may be only one way to satisfy those queries. Enter the forbidden ground of Indian legend and behold with your own eyes the powers of the vortex. Then only one more question will be left for you to answer—do you believe what your own eyes have seen?

CHAPTER 9

THE WALLOWA LAKE MONSTER

Oregon is blessed with an abundance of water. Many thousands of miles of streams and rivers drain its mountain ranges, while the landscape is dotted with lakes and reservoirs, from tiny mountain ponds just feet in diameter all the way up to Oregon's largest freshwater lake, the massive 61,543-acre Upper Klamath Lake, or the nation's deepest lake, at 1,932 feet, famed Crater Lake. As you might guess, these liquid assets also provide homes for a plethora of wild creatures. From frogs, turtles, and fish to beaver and otter, Oregon's waters host innumerable species of animals that either live in it or depend on its presence for food, drink, or a place to escape danger.

But stories are also told of other creatures that live in the deep, dark depths of a few lakes and rivers—creatures unknown to science, fearsome to look upon, and fatal to encounter up close. Some of these mysterious water beasts have long been known by Native American tribes, although in other instances the creatures have been discovered fairly recently. And those who have had the dubious opportunity to observe one of these large and frightening beasts as it rose suddenly from the depths have seldom expressed a desire to repeat the experience.

Humans have always believed that monsters dwelled on Earth, and nowhere was there a better lair for these unspeakable creatures than in the depths of the great, unknown sea. Often taking the form of a sea serpent (an animal combining the features of both a snake and a dragon), sea monsters were part of the lore of many cultures with ties to the ocean. Sightings of sea monsters go back to the ancient world and are prominent in Norse mythology. Some Native American tribes even had their own sea monster legends. One in particular is Gunakadeit, of the Tlingit tribe, who live along the Pacific Northwest coast of North America. Gunakadeit was a sea creature that brought prosperity and good fortune to any villagers who caught a glimpse of it. But compared to the Old World versions that ate cattle and sheep, sank ships, and swallowed hapless seafarers whole, Gunakadeit was an unusually benign sea monster.

But the world's oceans were not the only places that held water monsters. Reports, stories, and legends tell of similar creatures skulking about in large and remote lakes throughout the world. Undoubtedly the most famous lake monster is Scotland's Loch Ness monster, often affectionately referred to as Nessie. Nessie was first mentioned in a seventeenth-century book about Saint Columba of Ireland. The story in the book relates how one of Columba's companions went for a swim in the River Ness at

JIM YUSKAVITCH

Wallowa Lake in far northeastern Oregon is reputed to harbor a fierce water monster in its depths.

the head of the lake when a monster rose out of the water, bellowing and roaring, its mouth opened wide as if ready to swallow the terrified swimmer any moment. Columba stood on the banks, along with several other companions, watching this event transpire. Although the others stood frozen in fear, Columba ordered the beast to leave, making the sign of the cross as he did so, and the monster of the loch fled back to the depths, leaving the man in the water unscathed.

Sightings continue to this day—more than a thousand so far—and a few people have even managed to snap grainy photos of the beast, which many think is a holdover aquatic dinosaur. Although proof of Nessie's existence has yet to be proven, thousands of tourists flock to the shores of Loch Ness each year hoping to spot the legendary creature as it plies the lake's waters.

North America has its share of large lakes as well, along with its own indigenous lake monsters. Three of the most famous of these are Champ of Lake Champlain on the New York–Vermont border, and Canadian monsters Manipogo of Lake Manitoba and Ogopogo of Lake Okanagan.

Champ is reputed to reside in the waters of 535-square-mile Lake Champlain, which stretches for 125 miles from the Quebec border to Whitehall, New York. The legend of Champ goes back to the folklore of the Iroquois Indians who historically lived in the area and whose tribal traditions included a story about the great water creature that lived in the lake. The first "official" sighting of Champ was in 1883, and the beast was described as a "water serpent" about twenty-five to thirty feet long. Since then, more than three hundred people claim to have spotted the water monster of Lake Champlain.

Not to be outdone, Okanagan Lake, an 84-mile-long, 136-square-mile, 760-foot-deep water body in British Columbia's Okanagan Valley, also claims a water monster called Ogopogo. This serpentine creature, estimated to be about fifteen feet long, was first recorded in 1872 by early settlers to the area. In 1926 a crowd of more than thirty people reportedly saw the animal when it surfaced just off the beach where they were parked. In 1989 a man claimed to have filmed Ogopogo, but many people thought that the footage, showing a big splash as the creature dived below the surface, looked suspiciously like a beaver slapping its tail against the water. Nevertheless, true believers keep up the search.

Another big lake monster is Manipogo, named after the place in which it supposedly lives, 1,785-square-mile Lake Manitoba, located about fifty miles northwest of Winnipeg, Manitoba. Canada's thirty-third-largest lake, it's the perfect place for a water monster to hide out. People have been spotting it now and again since 1908 and describe it as similar in appearance to its cousin Ogopogo.

Water monsters—both saltwater and freshwater varieties—come in a range of shapes and sizes. The earliest reported sea monsters were long, slender, snakelike creatures with flaming red eyes and a mouth full of sharp, jagged teeth. Generally, they had large fins for swimming and sometimes dorsal fins as well. Those that didn't have fins may have sported a series of stiff or bony finlike structures down their backs, visible above the surface of the water as they swam in an undulating fashion. These monsters were reported to be up to two hundred feet long, such as the sea serpent of Norse legend that roamed off the coast of Norway and slunk onto land at night to feed on livestock but would eat humans just as readily.

But with a diversity of seas and lakes to occupy came a diversity of water monster types as well. Those include the classic slender, long-necked beasts, as well as a number of other body shapes. One kind was a snakelike but stout creature with a head that resembled a horse, with large eyes and whiskers. A many-humped beast is purported to live only in the North Atlantic Ocean, while another variety looks a bit like a sea lion but has a long neck and tail and may grow to lengths exceeding two hundred feet. Other water monsters are essentially gigantic versions of modern animals that we are familiar with, such as turtles, crocodiles, sharks, otters, manta rays, and squid.

Today, water monsters are more often than not described or depicted as a lizardlike animal with a stocky body, a long wedged tail, front and back flippers, and a head with tooth-laden jaws set at the end of a neck that is either slender and extended or short and thick—a profile that very much resembles a group of real creatures called plesiosaurs, which became extinct 65 million years ago.

Plesiosaurs were a group of saltwater-dwelling prehistoric aquatic reptiles that grew up to 660 feet long and are believed to have been the largest predators to have ever existed on planet Earth. They lived from the Triassic Period, 220 million years ago, until the Cretaceous Period, 65 million years ago, when they disappeared. During their time, plesiosaurs were a predator to be reckoned with. Their four paddlelike flippers propelled them efficiently and even elegantly through the water as they searched for the many small and strange creatures, such as belemnites and ammonites, that inhabited the ancient oceans and served as their prey. Some of the larger plesiosaurs probably also fed on smaller specimens of their own kind. Plesiosaurs, which swallowed their victims whole, had large rocks called gastroliths in their stomachs that literally ground up their food for digestion. The rocks also may have served as ballast to help the animals dive to great depths. In contrast to plesiosaurs, which had small heads and long slender necks, the closely related and equally fierce pliosaurs had large heads and thick, short necks.

Plesiosaur fossils were first discovered in England in 1820, at a time when the idea of the existence of dinosaurs was relatively new. These were among the first prehistoric fossils to be studied systematically by scientists. In addition to England, fossil plesiosaurs and pliosaurs have been discovered in Australia, Mexico, South America, North America, and the Scandinavian Arctic.

The popular view of water monsters as plesiosaurs, or other species of aquatic dinosaurs that have somehow managed to survive into modern times, may have started with the release of the 1933 blockbuster film *King Kong*. The movie included a scene of something resembling a plesiosaur rising out of a large lake, thus introducing dinosaurs to popular culture. The following year the famous photograph of the Loch Ness monster, a long-necked sea beast with a humped back, was published in the *London Daily Mail*, causing a worldwide sensation. Since then, water monsters and plesiosaurs have been inextricably linked.

Many water monster legends can trace their roots to Native American mythology, which in some cases may actually be based on scientific fact. Take the Lakota Sioux legend of the Wakinyan (Thunder Beings) and Unktehila (water monsters).

The Thunder Beings represented good and provided rain, thunder, and lightning that brought life to Earth, while the water monsters represented evil. The evil Unktehila were reptilian in nature and destroyed all life in their path, so the Wakinyan were compelled to attack them in an attempt to make the world safe for all beings. Eventually, a great battle was fought, and the Thunder Beings rained lightning down upon the water monsters until they were killed and their lakes dried up. While the Wakinyan were victorious, some Unktehila survived but shrank in size, and all that remain of them are the small lizards and snakes we know today.

But the Sioux's idea of gigantic water-dwelling reptiles is not as fanciful as it might seem. Some 250 million years ago, the northern plains area where the Sioux and other tribes lived was a great shallow sea that was populated by prehistoric aquatic animals, including plesiosaurs. The Indians were known to have occasionally stumbled upon the fossilized remains of these ancient sea-dwelling creatures, which not only furnished proof in their minds that the stories of the Wakinyan and the Unktehila were true but also probably gave rise to the original legend as well.

Further indication that the indigenous peoples of the North American grasslands were aware of the previous existence of dinosaurs is found in dinosaur likenesses painted on the tee-pee covers of a number of Plains Indian tribes, including the Blackfeet, Cheyenne, and Kiowa. Petroglyphs depicting these creatures can also be found on cliffs along the Missouri River.

NICOLLE RAGER, NATIONAL SCIENCE FOUNDATION

Artist's rendition of a plesiosaur, a common prehistoric sea creature that some believe still exists in deep, remote lakes.

Whether classic sea serpents or remnant plesiosaurs, strange and fearsome monsters are said to be lurking in the waters of Oregon—both fresh and salt. The granddaddy sea monster that purportedly skulks along Oregon's coast, as well as the coasts of Washington, British Columbia, and Alaska, is known as Caddy. According to reports, it is about fifteen feet long, snakelike, with humps on its back, and swims in an undulating motion. Caddy also sports a forked tail that makes it resemble a whale when it is diving.

Two other sea monsters have been reported off the Oregon coast—Colossal Claude and Marvin the Monster. Claude was first sighted in 1934 at the mouth of the Columbia River by the crewmen of a Columbia River lightship (a permanently moored ship that has a beacon mounted on it and serves as a floating lighthouse). It was reported to be forty feet long, with a long neck, a fat body, and "a mean looking tail and an evil, snaky look to its head." Claude was spotted again three years later and then popped up from time to time for a while thereafter.

A crew of divers working for the Shell Oil Company supposedly saw Marvin in 1963 off the Oregon coast, although exactly where isn't clear. Marvin was also rumored to have been filmed at this time, but the whereabouts of that footage are unknown.

Occasionally, remains of a sea monster wash up onshore, creating a sensation, as was reported to have happened at Delake (now part of Lincoln City) in March 1950. Said to have been twenty-two feet long and weighing around a thousand pounds, the carcass was so badly decomposed that it was never positively identified.

This is a common situation with sea monster remains, which are referred to as globsters because they are usually an unidentifiable mass of tissue of a dead and decaying sea animal. If some recognizable parts, such as tails, fins, and jaws, are still attached, it may give the appearance of a fantastical unknown creature. Often, globsters turn out to be decomposing whales or sharks. Dead whale sharks that have washed ashore are common culprits in cases of sea monster mistaken identity. In death, the heads and tails of these large—up to forty feet long—plankton-eating sharks tend to decompose first; what remains looks like it might be a plesiosaur carcass.

Coincidentally, just a stone's throw from the ocean in Lincoln City, where the half-ton mystery globster drifted ashore in 1950, is Devil's Lake, which is rumored to harbor its own water monster. According to a local Indian legend, a certain Chief Fleetfoot one dark night was paddling across the lake on his way to a romantic liaison on the far shore. But halfway across, a fearsome monster with octopus-like tentacles rose from the lake's depths, grasped the canoe and the terrified, shrieking Indian, and dragged him below the surface along with his craft.

Another Oregon lake monster—or in this case, a devil story that comes down from Native American legends—centers on Crater Lake. Located in the Cascade Mountains in southern Oregon and now protected within a national park, Crater Lake remained unknown to white people until a group of prospectors out hunting stumbled upon it on June 12, 1853.

But the local Indians, primarily the Klamath people, knew about the place for thousands of years. Formed by a tremendous volcanic eruption about 6,600 years ago, Crater Lake covers 13,139 acres and is nearly 2,000 feet deep. When white people finally found the lake, they viewed it as a wonder of nature. Native Americans knew it as a place of great spiritual power and great danger. Shamans, the only people spiritually strong enough to visit the lake safely, would go there to seek visions. All others trespassed on this sacred ground at their own peril.

The reason for fear was that spirits who did the bidding of Llao, the Klamath Indian name for the "god of the world below," guarded the lake zealously. These "lake devils" often took the form of tiny humans or animals and attacked interlopers on Llao's command. In the lake there roamed another creature, a large octopus-like monster, said to be Llao himself, accompanied by smaller look-alike minions. One story from the Klamath tribes relates that, many years ago, a Klamath warrior, despite knowing better, went down to the lake and caught and killed a huge fish. Enraged at this transgression, dozens of lake devils swarmed out from the water and captured the warrior. As he struggled to free himself from their terrible grasp, they carried him to the top of the cliffs that encircle the lake and slit his throat with a knife. Next they tore his body into tiny pieces and tossed those pieces into the lake, where they were devoured by more lake devils waiting below. To this day, many Klamath Indians still consider Crater Lake to be a sacred place and a potentially hazardous one for the spiritually unprepared.

Although most water monsters live in the sea or large, deep lakes, Oregon has the distinction of playing host to a rare river-dwelling creature in the form of the serpent of the Illinois River, one of the major streams of the southwestern part of the state. It was first sighted in the winter of 1881. Sometimes during that season, heavy rains in the mountains would flood the river, and its raging waters would carry big logs from the forest downstream. Area homesteaders often went out on the river during these high-flow periods to salvage the logs, which provided good wood for many construction and repair projects.

That winter, a group of men were out on the river in boats collecting this bounty. During the course of the salvage operation, one of the men leapt upon an especially large log, his cork boots sinking into the bark's surface. But to his great astonishment, the log erupted from the river, dumped him into the water, and made a beeline upstream. The others rescued the man from the water, but they were thoroughly spooked. Once they had pulled him to safety, they all went home to ponder what they had observed. Whatever the creature was, they guessed it to be at least two hundred feet long.

Late that night, a cow from one of the riverside homesteads went missing from a pasture, and the next night a horse vanished. Another farmer lost twelve hogs. Reports of missing livestock circulated up and down the river. Then, as spring arrived, the depredations ceased. But the following winter the creature was back, and a farmer even spotted it basking on a gravel bar. It was described as having a snake's body, mostly brown, but its head was blue with red and yellow spots. It had a single horn on its head, and out of its mouth flickered a forked tongue. It was seen numerous times that winter, and homesteaders took many shots at it, to no ill effect.

Finally, a farmer volunteered to use an old bull ox as bait, thinking that the animal's large horns would be too wide for the serpent to swallow and it would choke to death on them. The farmer and his companions herded the ox out onto a gravel bar by the river where the serpent lay, and it immediately swallowed the hapless animal. But, as predicted, it couldn't open its jaws quite wide enough to gulp down the horns. Several days later, the serpent was seen still struggling to swallow, and eventually it swam downriver and presumably out to sea. The serpent was never seen again, although from time to time fishermen have reported glimpsing similar creatures on the river, and some think a family group may live somewhere in the remote headwaters.

But Oregon's most famous water monster hides in the depths of Wallowa Lake, a beautiful 1,508-acre glacial lake set in a spectacular alpine setting located just a few miles south of Joseph in the far northeastern corner of the state. The fearsome creature is known as the Wallowa Lake monster, and it was familiar to the Nez Percé Indians who once lived in the Wallowa Valley and whose stories about it first alerted white settlers to the creature that lived in their midst. Perhaps that information was not a great surprise to the local farmers and ranchers. Although Wallowa Lake is known to be almost 300 feet deep at its deepest point and averages about 160 feet in depth, for many years it was regarded as "bottomless," sparking speculation among area residents about what strange things might reside in its limitless depths.

While there are several versions of the tale of the Wallowa Lake monster, the most noted one was told by a young Nez Percé warrior named Joseph, who would later become a famous chief among his people. Joseph narrated the story to a pioneer named George A. Waggoner in the 1860s as he passed through the Wallowa Valley.

In Waggoner's account, he and his party were camped near Wallowa Lake, where they met a group of six Nez Percé Indians, including Joseph, who were out elk hunting. The Indians invited the white men along, and they readily accepted. The day's hunt was wildly successful, bagging thirteen of the massive animals, plenty of meat for both parties. Before continuing on, Waggoner and his group camped in the area for several days as they dried the elk meat for their journey. During that time Joseph visited their camp several times, and on one visit he decided to tell his new white friends a little history about the nearby lake.

It was the custom of the Nez Percé to make periodic journeys east to the plains to hunt buffalo. These expeditions brought them into the territory of the Blackfeet Indians, a strong and warlike tribe, and occasionally battles were fought between the two peoples. About two hundred years before, as Joseph told it, one such battle was fought under the leadership of a chief named Red Wolf. In this particular fight the Nez Percé suffered a stunning defeat and lost many of their warriors. Limping back to the Wallowa Valley and their camp by Wallowa Lake, they set about recovering from their losses. But during another battle the following winter, the tables were turned, and it was the Nez Percé who were the victors.

But the Blackfeet eventually sent a large war party to the Wallowa Valley to seek revenge. They camped on Wallowa Lake directly across from the Nez Percé village so that they could easily strike and then return to their camp to prepare for more attacks.

The two tribes fought back and forth for many days, and slowly the Blackfeet were gaining the upper hand. So many Nez Percé warriors were killed that the tribe found itself at real risk of annihilation.

Desperate, Red Wolf's daughter Wahluna slipped out of camp one dark night and canoed across the lake to the enemy camp. There she presented herself to the Blackfoot chief and pleaded her case. She said that there were only women, old men, and children in her camp. Without warriors to fight, there was no honor in battle, so the Blackfeet had no need to attack.

The chief of the Blackfeet agreed not to attack. After the appropriate ceremony with the surviving Nez Percé to seal the deal, the Blackfeet packed up and went back to their own country on the plains. But before the Blackfeet left, Wahluna and Tlesca, the son of the Blackfoot chief, fell in love, and arrangements were made for the two tribes to meet along the lake in six months for the wedding.

The wedding was one to remember in tribal history, not just for the grandness of the ceremonies, singing, dancing, and food, which included buffalo from the plains and trout from the lake, but also for what happened afterward.

As dusk began to settle and the sunset caused the lake and mountains to shimmer in an array of vibrant reds and yellows, the happy couple decided to take a short canoe ride across the lake's still waters. Guests gathered on the bank and watched the two newlyweds shove off and quietly paddle away. Suddenly, to their horror, they watched as a great serpent rose out of the water and overturned the canoe, spilling Wahluna and Tlesca into the drink, where they promptly disappeared. Occasional sightings of one or more Wallowa Lake monsters—locally known as Wally— have been reported ever since.

Descriptions of the Wallowa Lake monster vary, but it is often said to look something like a traditional Chinese dragon, with a single horn on its forehead and a series of humps on its back; other witnesses say it resembles a buffalo. Its length reportedly is as small as eight feet or as large as seventy-five feet.

The earliest recorded sighting of the monster was reported in the November 5, 1885, edition of the *Wallowa County Chieftain,* the local Joseph newspaper. One evening a prospector was on the lake in a skiff. As he reached the middle of the lake, he spotted some kind of aquatic animal about fifty yards away. It raised its head ten or twelve feet out of the water and then dived beneath the surface when it noticed the man in the boat. The prospector described the strange beast as having a large, flat head, similar to that of a hippopotamus, and said that it bellowed softly, sounding somewhat like a cow. The prospector, fearing ridicule, refused to allow his name to be revealed to the public.

In 1932 local resident Bob Reese and his wife reported seeing a "large fish" in the lake that was longer than their eleven-foot boat. They were a few hundred yards off the west shore, and the creature was hovering near the bottom. They couldn't get a good look at it, but they continually circled over the curious-looking animal and reported that it ignored them the entire time. In the mid-1940s the owner of one of the tourist lodges on the lake claimed to have seen "a big black thing, like a hogs head" swimming on the lake as she was out horseback riding one day. The creature swam off, bobbing up and down before vanishing from sight.

Then, in 1950, local residents H. C. Wicklander and his wife, along with Joe Tatone, who was visiting from Portland, spotted two of the monsters. One was about eight feet long, and the other was about twice that size. They were feeding on the landlocked salmon that inhabit Wallowa Lake and that some think make up the monsters' primary food source. Except for the unlucky Indian newlyweds of Nez Percé legend, no other attacks by the Wallowa Lake monster on humans have ever been reported, although it is said that drowning victims whose bodies are never recovered were likely carried off by the creature.

As for whether the monster of Wallowa Lake really exists, you might take note of what the original Nez Percé storyteller, Joseph, thought about the matter. When the tale was done, pioneer George Waggoner leaned forward and asked the Indian if he really believed that a huge serpent swallowed up Wahluna and Tlesca on their fateful wedding night. The future chief purportedly said, without needing to give it much thought, "No. One big wind, one big wave, that's all." Still, what lies in the deep, dark depths of the boundless ocean or in remote and foreboding lakes will always pique the human imagination, and if fish and whales aren't enough, we are just as likely to fill that mysterious and unknown place with fearsome monsters.

CHAPTER 10

PORTLAND, SHANGHAI CITY

The three sailors debarked from their ship with a mind to spend their several days of shore leave taking in the entertainment and sights offered by the rough-and-tumble riverfront district of Portland known in the late 1800s as Slabtown because so many of its denizens ended up on a slab in the city morgue. Unfortunately, they had little cash between them, certainly not enough to pay for a few nights at the Slabtown boardinghouse where they had stopped to inquire about a room. Cash-strapped sailors in town was nothing unusual, for captains often held off paying sailors until they had completed their service, lest they be tempted to desert ship at the next port of call. But lack of money would be no problem on this night, for the kindly boarding-house owner was a friend to all hardworking sailors and would gladly put them up for a few nights on credit. He even treated them to a couple of beers to quench their thirst.

Twenty-four hours later, the knockout drops with which their ales had been spiked were wearing off. As the three sailors slowly regained consciousness, they found themselves shackled in the hold of a deepwater sailing ship, now well out to sea. As the fog of the drugs dissipated, they came to the realization that they had been shanghaied—kidnapped from their ship and sold to a captain in need of a crew, whose original crew may also have been shanghaied. Now far from the sight of land, the three had little choice but to sign on as crew and hope that it would not be too many years before they saw their home port again.

Shanghaiing—or "crimping," as it was commonly called—was the brutal and vile practice of supplying commercial sailing ships with experienced crews, by trickery and violence, when there were not enough able-bodied seamen willing to volunteer or when a captain's crew members deserted or were themselves shanghaied by crimps, as practitioners of this evil trade were dubbed. The practice was common at seaports along both coasts of America, but from the mid-1800s to the early 1900s, it was especially prevalent on the West Coast. Portland was known as one of the most active centers of the crimping business, and a most dangerous port of call for the common sailor. Rumor even has it that much of this unsavory business was conducted in a dark labyrinth of tunnels that ran beneath Slabtown.

Shanghaiing has its roots in the British practice of impressment. Dating back to the mid-1500s, impressment involved kidnapping young men with seafaring skills and forcing them to serve in the British navy against their will. Although an

official Impressment Ser-
vice oversaw such "recruitment," a ship of the Royal
Navy in need of additional
manpower might, acting
on its own, intercept a
merchant ship, board it,
and impress a number of
its crew. Unlike crimp-
ing, British law allowed
impressed sailors who felt
they were unfairly taken
to appeal to a court of
law, and many times they
prevailed in their argu-
ments, especially if they

OREGON STATE ARCHIVES

*Joseph "Bunco" Kelly was one
of the most notorious of the
Portland crimps.*

had little sailing experience. It was a wartime practice meant to
fill recruitment shortages exclusively in the Royal Navy and was
ended in 1814.

As with impressment, shanghaiing also came about because
of a shortage of skilled merchant sailors, especially on the West
Coast of the United States. The practice began in the 1850s when
ships' crews deserted by the thousands to seek their fortunes in
the goldfields of California and Oregon. This left a dearth of
qualified seamen to man the deepwater wind-powered ships that
transported various trade goods between U.S. and foreign ports.

In stepped the crimps to fill this demand. Crimps were usually associated with boardinghouses that catered to sailors, either as owners of the establishment themselves or in partnership with boardinghouse owners. Working out of boardinghouses put the crimps in a position to make money off itinerant merchant sailors in a number of ways.

The most straightforward and commonly used method was kidnapping, employing either guile or force, but kidnapping it was nonetheless. The simplest, but most risky, method was for several crimps to accost a sailor on the street late at night, overpower him with billy clubs and brass-knuckled fists, gag and tie him, and put him in the crimps' boardinghouse basement for safekeeping. Another often-used approach was to befriend a group of sailors on shore leave and then render them unconscious with a sedative placed in their drinks. Crimps often used chloral hydrate, a sedative that was first concocted in 1832 by German chemist Justus von Liebig. Chloral hydrate, which is manufactured from ethanol and chlorine mixed in an acidic solution, easily dissolves in both water and alcohol, so it made the perfect "knockout drop" for the crimps' purposes. Sailors snared this way also ended up bound and gagged in a safe location until it was time to ship them out.

In another equally nefarious but less forceful technique, a group of crimps would approach a ship at dock and talk the crew into deserting with promises of better pay and working conditions with a job onshore, with which they would happily set them up. It was an effective technique. Between 1896 and 1900, more than 2,100 British sailors deserted their ships at Portland, most of them from the influence of crimps.

The crimps generally backed up these one-sided negotiations with large-caliber revolvers in case the ship's captain expressed any objections. If the crew was enticed off the ship, everyone made for the crimps' boardinghouse to celebrate with drinks. After the sailors drank themselves into a stupor, they eventually awoke on board another ship, victims of a shanghaiing. Meanwhile, the captain who had lost his crew would have to buy a new one from the crimps at inflated prices. Some crimps even had the audacity to try to hold the original crew's captain financially liable for the liquor used to shanghai them.

On the other hand, sometimes a ship's captain would actively encourage his crew to desert by refusing to pay any advances on their wages or by deliberately creating harsh conditions on board. The idea was to get the sailors to abandon ship before they were paid, saving the ship's owners a good deal of money. Then the captain could "recruit" a new crew with help from the local crimps, after dumping his former sailors onto the docks and making them ripe for shanghaiing to another ship. It was a good deal all around, except for the seamen, since the law at the time allowed captains to refuse to pay sailors who left their employ before their contract was up, even for work already performed.

As profitable as it was, shanghaiing wasn't necessarily the only or even the most lucrative way to bilk money from sailors and ship's captains alike. One especially productive scam manipulated the way captains paid their crews to the crimps' benefit.

It was common practice, especially on British ships, for the captain to pay his crew only a small percentage of their pay before they had completed their full enlistment lest they be tempted to desert. As a result, sailors on shore leave were always short on funds. Crimps who owned boardinghouses took advantage of their plight with a simple entrapment scheme by offering them credit for lodging, food, drink, and whatever else they might desire. Then, when the sailor had rung up a substantial debt, the crimps would put him on a ship that needed a crew, whether he wanted to go or not, with his seaman's salary going to the crimp to settle the debt.

Some ship's captains provided their crew with a small advance to purchase a few personal items and tools for an upcoming voyage. But instead of cash, they would agree to directly pay the merchant who sold the seamen these items. The crimps cashed in on this arrangement by selling the merchandise to the sailors at grossly inflated prices and then collecting from their captains.

All in all, a good crimp could make out pretty well. Money paid to the crimps for shanghaied sailors, called "blood money," ranged from $25 to $135 or more, depending on how desperate a captain was for a crew. Typically the captains were desperate, for when they suddenly lost a crew at port, it was often the doings of the local crimps. Blood money generally averaged between $50 and $75 per man. This, along with the other schemes and scams the crimps played on ship's captains and crews, added up. Some crimps in the late 1800s were reported to have made as much as $9,500 per year, the equivalent of more than $200,000 in today's currency. That kind of money permitted the more prominent crimps to buy friends in high places, including policemen who looked the other way and politicians who blocked anti-shanghaiing legislation.

From the 1870s to the 1920s, when shanghaiing ran rampant, Portland was an important and growing port town, especially for exporting wheat, wool, and salmon. Ships would load their cargo on Portland's Willamette River waterfront and then transport it

Portland was one of the most dangerous ports of call on the West Coast because of the high level of shanghaiing activity that took place there between the mid-1800s and the 1920s. Pictured is the bark Emanuel Accane *docked at Portland Harbor about 1907.*

down the Columbia to Astoria, another center of shanghaiing, where it was shipped to markets in Asia and other destinations. Nearly 100,000 tons of wheat worth more than $3.1 million was shipped out of Portland in 1876 alone. It was a far cry from just three decades earlier, when Portland was merely a meadow in the forest known as "the clearing" with just a few lonely pioneers living in small log cabins nearby.

In the 1890s on the West Coast, wherever you found a busy port full of sailors, you also found crimps. Portland, Oregon, was the exception only in that the practice of shanghaiing was more blatant and brutal than anywhere else. Crimping was concentrated in Slabtown—today known as the Old Town and Chinatown areas.

Portland had a number of notable crimps, including Peter Grant, Jim Vierck, J. P. Betts, David Evans, and Billy Smith. But a few were more famous, and effective, than the others. First and foremost was Larry Sullivan, whom many considered to be the "king" of the Portland crimps. He operated a boardinghouse on the corner of Second and Glisan Streets and was also prominent in the local boxing scene. Sullivan reputedly was less inclined to use violence and relied more on persuasion in obtaining sailors, but he didn't shy away from using alcohol mixed with knockout drops if that's what it took.

Like any gangs, crimps were constantly at war with one another for territory and access to docked ships. In one incident in 1890 or 1891, local crimp Billy Smith had a knock-down-drag-out fight with Sullivan on Second Street, bloodied him up pretty good, and walked away the winner. The victor in such tussles generally won some or all of the loser's territory. But in this case, the two savvy crimps decided that it was in their best interest to join forces instead, leading to one of the most celebrated shanghaiing stories of Portland lore.

In October 1891 twenty-one-year-old Aquilla Ernest Clark arrived in Portland from one of the surrounding farm communities. He was looking to experience the adventures of the big city when he had the misfortune to bump into one of Sullivan and Smith's runners, men who introduced themselves to anyone on the street who looked like a candidate for shanghaiing and chatted him up with offers of a place to stay, food, drink, a good-paying job, or anything else that might put the hapless mark in their clutches. In this case, the runner helpfully advised Clark that the best place to stay in town was at the sailors' boarding-house on the corner of Second and Glisan, which just happened to be owned by Larry Sullivan. Clark rented a room and found a number of other men also staying at Sullivan's boardinghouse, offering plenty of company and conversation through the evening hours.

The next morning, Billy Smith greeted the boardinghouse guests with a cheerful "good morning" and an offer to buy them all breakfast. Over the morning repast Smith mentioned that his business associate, Larry Sullivan, had chartered a riverboat for a day trip to Astoria and back, and Smith suggested that they come along. There would be music, liquor, and attractive young ladies to make the trip that much more interesting. Clark and eight other guests jumped at the invitation.

Upon boarding the riverboat *Iralda*, the men were handed a glass of peach blow fizz, a cocktail consisting of gin, cream, lemon juice, carbonated water, and peaches and said to have been invented by the manager of the Portland Hotel. As the *Iralda* made its way downriver, a three-piece band hired by Sullivan struck up dance music as the women on board dragged their guests onto the deck, which became an impromptu dance floor. Smith circulated around, chatting amicably, telling stories, and making everyone feel comfortable. Dinner was a feast of steak, pork, oysters, crab, and salmon, and the whiskey, rum, and wine flowed copiously.

By the time the *Iralda* reached Astoria, about a hundred miles downstream from Portland at the Pacific Ocean, Clark and his eight companions were beginning to feel a little woozy from all the alcohol they had drunk. Now the trap was beginning to close. Smith approached each man with a sheet of paper and pen, explaining that everyone was going ashore at Astoria for an hour of sightseeing and that they needed to sign their names so that when it was time to depart for the return trip to Portland, he could take a head count and match it to the passenger list to ensure that no one would be left behind. They all dutifully signed the paper.

The men went ashore, mostly imbibing at the local taverns. After a half hour or so, Smith asked his guests if they would like to see a real deepwater sailing ship. None of them being sailors, they agreed, thinking it would be interesting to have a look. Out they rowed to the *T. F. Oakes,* a ship notorious for the cruel treatment its captain meted out to his crew and for the poor and unhealthful conditions on board.

The instant the men climbed aboard, they were accosted at gunpoint by the captain and Smith, marched belowdecks, and chained in the hold. Once out at sea, the men were released, brought topside, and put to work. They had been shanghaied, and the paper they had signed was not a passenger list at all, but an agreement to serve as crew on the hell ship *T. F. Oakes.*

Sullivan, who was also active in local Portland politics for the purpose of protecting his business interests, used some innovative techniques to influence elections. In one case, he paid a crew of Dutch sailors $2 each to vote for the candidate of Sullivan's choice and with a shotgun chased off a police officer who had arrived at the polls to investigate claims of potential voter fraud. Sullivan's politician friends made sure he suffered no charges for that incident. Sullivan was known to brag that "he was the law in Portland."

Over the years, as ship's masters and owners began to increasingly protest the depredations of Portland crimps, Sullivan's political connections continually paid off. In one case, the captain of the *Dunstaffnage* lodged an official complaint that Sullivan was demanding $135 per man for a crew, far too much. The police arrested Sullivan and fined him $50. But his political friends stepped in, and when they were done, the captain of the *Dunstaffnage* was required to pay Sullivan his $135 per man rate along with Sullivan's fine before the ship was allowed to sail. Sullivan even sued a captain who had the nerve to publicly criticize him and his crimping activities for criminal and civil libel. The captain was able to sneak out of town and stowed on board another ship, avoiding a trial whose verdict would likely have been rigged.

Such incidents were extremely vexing to the owners of shipping companies. Yet for a time, when Sullivan's crimping empire was at its most powerful, ship's captains were told not to bother resisting the Portland gang's terms as it was too dangerous to defy Sullivan and no help could be expected from the local authorities.

Sullivan, after a lengthy criminal career in Portland, died in 1918 at about the age of fifty-five. He is buried in the city's Mount Calvary Cemetery.

At six feet tall and two hundred pounds, dressed in a suit, and carrying a gold-topped cane, crimp Jim Turk was a striking figure along the Portland docks in the early 1890s. His boardinghouse beckoned the unwary on Couch Street, between First and Second Streets. Previously a partner in a Pendleton saloon, Turk eventually moved to Astoria and got into the crimping business there before bringing his entrepreneurial skill for shanghaiing to Portland.

Astoria, on the Pacific Ocean at the mouth of the Columbia River, was almost as nefarious a port for shanghaiing as was Portland. What it lacked in organization and political clout compared to Portland, it made up for in brutality. In the early 1880s crimps in Astoria boldly combed the countryside and backwoods for victims, kidnapping men right out of their cabins, giving them a good beating to quiet them down, binding them, and shipping them off to crew a Shanghai-bound ship. In one especially egregious case in the 1880s, several crimps attempted to shanghai the city's Methodist minister, George Grannis, right out of his own church. Fortunately, Grannis put up enough of a struggle, combined with some amateur boxing skills, to send his would-be abductors packing. One left a few teeth behind. Crimping could be a dangerous business in Astoria, and occasionally rival crimps shot each other dead in broad daylight.

Some claim that Jim Turk actually introduced shanghaiing to the West Coast. Whether or not that is true, Turk was known to be a bully and a brute. He's most famous for shanghaiing his own son, ostensibly for bad behavior involving liquor and women. Turk collected the blood money, of course, when he handed his son off to the ship's captain. It was also said that Turk once shanghaied a Portland doctor. But when the doctor returned, instead of pressing charges, he thanked the crimp for his services. It seems that the doctor suffered from tuberculosis, and his time in the fresh sea air apparently cured him.

But far from the fresh air of the open sea was the Portland Underground, made up of dark, dank basements, belowground loading docks, cisterns, and, some claim, a network of tunnels, snaking beneath Portland. According to legend, it was in this dark netherworld where most shanghaiing took place, with crimps hustling their bound and drugged captives off to safekeeping in cellars deep beneath the city streets and then hustling them back to the docks and onto a waiting ship via the tunnels. Even more diabolical were trap doors strategically placed in various bars, boardinghouses, and hotels. Unsuspecting and drunk or drugged sailors on shore leave and rubes visiting from the backwoods would find the floor suddenly dropping beneath their feet, sending them into the clutches of the crimps waiting below.

In fact, there are old basements and cisterns underneath Portland's Old Town, along with underground passageways near the river. Although these might have been used for shanghaiing from time to time, their main purposes were for transporting cargo to and from ships, flood control, and drainage. Shanghaiing was so tolerated by Portland authorities that the crimps hardly needed to be so secretive.

Ladies of the night, a prominent fixture in Portland's seedy waterfront district, may have played a small role in shanghaiing since brothels were a popular destination for sailors, longshoremen, and the many other characters who roamed this less respectable part of the city. One of the more well-known madams of the day was Nancy Boggs, who built her house of ill repute on a scow on the Willamette River, where some shanghaiing might have taken place. Boggs was particularly clever to locate her enterprise on water. When Boggs's informants warned her that a police raid was imminent, she simply steamed off across the river and out of the law's jurisdiction. On the other hand, the madam Elizabeth Smith, more widely known as Liverpool Liz, ran the land-bound Senate Saloon on Second Street and was more likely to protect sailors than to take advantage of them. She was known to help people on the outs with food and to put drunken sailors' valuables in safekeeping until they were in a condition to take responsibility again.

The most famous Portland crimp, by far, was Joseph "Bunco" Kelly. In addition to using the usual tried-and-true shanghaiing methods, Kelly won a name for himself for a couple of especially notable instances of creative crimping.

As the story has it, the captain of the *Warwick*, a British ship that had put into Portland to take on a cargo of lumber bound for Australia, was one crewman short. Knowing Kelly's reputation as a crimp who could "recruit" a sailor from the Portland waterfront in short order, the captain looked him up at his boardinghouse, the Mariner's Home, on Third and Davis. After some haggling, the captain agreed to the usurious fee of $200, half to be paid in advance and the remainder upon delivery of the goods.

The deal made, Kelly stole off into the dark streets of Portland with partner Stingaree Poe. The two trolled the waterfront for a likely prospect, but after long hours of searching they could find neither a sailor they could talk into willingly signing on to the *Warwick* nor one drunk enough to shanghai. In desperation,

Kelly had an idea. He and Poe made their way to a nearby tobacco shop and absconded with the wooden Indian that stood out front. Next, they turned their wooden Indian into a sailor with the addition of a sou'wester hat stretched over the war bonnet and a pair of rubber boots to hide moccasined feet. Then they wrapped the whole package up in an oilskin coat. When they hauled their catch onto the *Warwick,* their explanation that the man was drunk and only needed a few hours to sleep it off in a quiet corner of the ship apparently satisfied the captain, who paid Kelly and Poe the remaining $100 as agreed. The two walked down the ship's gangplank, probably doing their best to keep from laughing out loud and giving their scam away. Ever since that night, Joseph Kelly became "Bunco" Kelly in honor of the great trick he played on the captain of the *Warwick.*

Kelly was also involved in one of the grimmer Portland shanghaiing incidents. One night in October 1893, as Kelly was stalking the streets in search of sailors to fill an order, he heard the low mumble of voices emanating from the basement of an adjacent building. Noticing an open trap door, he cautiously ventured down to investigate. Upon entering the basement, he was met with a horrifying sight—two dozen men lying on the floor, fourteen of whom were dead and the rest gravely ill. Never one to miss a moneymaking opportunity, Kelly sent a boy to get a cab and a few men to help with some heavy lifting. When assistance and transportation arrived, Kelly and his helpers loaded them all up and made for the docks.

Finding the *Flying Prince* dockside and in need of a crew, he sold the men to the captain for $30 each, explaining that all were drunk and would sober up eventually. All twenty-four were carried on board, including the fourteen bodies, and the captain set sail down the Columbia toward the sea. By the time he made Astoria, they were all dead. The captain off-loaded the bodies and took on a new and livelier crew—in all likelihood supplied by the local crimps.

What killed the men? It seems that the group—whether they were sailors is not known—were out looking for a good time. Noticing the open basement trap door, as did Kelly, they went down to see what it might hold. What they found were two large kegs sitting on the floor. The men apparently believed they were in the basement of the Snug Harbor Saloon, facing a golden opportunity to drink the beer in those kegs for free. Unfortunately, the men had actually wandered into the basement of a mortuary, and the kegs were filled with formaldehyde. It didn't take long for them to drink themselves, literally, to death.

Kelly also held the speed crimping record, once shanghai-ing fifty men and hustling them on board a four-masted bark in barely three hours' time.

Kelly was eventually convicted of killing a man named George W. Sayers while attempting to shanghai him in 1894 (although some believe he was framed and was actually engaged in a fight with Larry Sullivan at the time of the murder). He spent thirteen years in the Oregon State Penitentiary, where he wrote a book about his experiences. Upon his release he moved to southern California.

But the days of the crimps, not only in Portland but also in the port towns up and down the West Coast, were numbered. As the crimps became bolder in their scams against ship's masters and crews, the outrage of the shipping company owners increased as well. Political pressure to rein in the crimps intensified, and a variety of laws were passed for that purpose. Finally, with the passage of the Seaman's Act of 1915, which was essentially a "bill of rights" for sailors, forcible recruitment as well as other cruel treatments and conditions on board ships became illegal, and shanghaiing eventually disappeared.

But shanghaiing was so embedded in Portland's waterfront economy that it reportedly lasted into the 1920s—well after the practice had vanished from the rest of the West Coast. What finally killed shanghaiing were technology and the laws of supply and demand. As steamboats replaced sailing ships, smaller and less skilled crews were the norm. And because the Seaman's Act improved working conditions for sailors, they were less likely to desert, and consequently captains' demand for crews began falling. As a result of these developments, the crimps' services were no longer needed, and they went out of business. A cruel and violent period of American maritime history vanished with them.

CHAPTER 11

PIRATE TREASURES BURIED, HAUNTED, AND CURSED

Although tales of treasure, buried and otherwise, seem most appropriate for desert isles set in tropical seas where pirates roamed and plundered, Oregon has its share of alleged deadman's chests brimming with gold doubloons and other caches of valuables hidden long ago for mysterious reasons by unknown persons who never returned to claim their ill-gotten property.

With the wild north Pacific Ocean pounding against Oregon's western boundary, and sundry ships visiting its shores over the past several centuries, it should come as no surprise that stories of riches hidden by wandering seafarers have been passed down through word of mouth over the years by early white settlers and even as part of the lore of local Native American tribes.

One such tale goes back to the early 1930s, when one E. G. Calkins and a group of workers were sifting and raking the sand on Three Rocks Beach, located in Lincoln County where the Salmon River empties into the sea. The object of their task was to make a smooth, comfortable camping area for the summer tourists who would soon be arriving for some relaxation and rec-reation along the coast. Calkins, a former Lincoln County com-missioner, was well aware of the important contribution tourism made to the local economy, and he was happy to personally lend a hand to make sure visitors had an enjoyable experience.

As the men labored to clear away driftwood, garbage, and other detritus washed ashore by the relentless waves to make spaces for the many camping tents they hoped would soon be pitched there, they also came across other, more interesting objects. Some of those objects included old iron kettles, stone grinding pestles, and even a club made of whale bone, along with piles of old seashells. However, to the men working on the beach, these finds were routine, as it was well known that Native American tribes regularly camped in this area as long ago as per-haps four thousand years, using it as a base for food-gathering activities. As a result, there were large shell middens, along with various artifacts that had been lost or discarded by those long-ago campers. The site, besides being a prime camping spot for harried city dwellers looking to get away for a while, was also an old Indian garbage dump.

Then, one of the men cried out that he had found some-thing different and unexpected and called the others over to have a look. There, lying in the overturned sand, was a human thighbone. As the other workers gathered round, it occurred to them that this was a historical Indian campsite, not a burial ground, so this discovery merited further investigation. Wielding

HOWARD PYLE, *HOWARD PYLE'S BOOK OF PIRATES*, 1921

Pirates killing one of their number and leaving his ghost to guard their treasure is a common element in tales of buried pirate loot.

their picks and shovels, they began digging in the vicinity where the thighbone was found. Before long, they made an even more astonishing discovery—two complete human skeletons. One skeleton was particularly astonishing because it belonged to a man who was nearly eight feet tall.

Lugging their archaeological finds back to civilization, Calkins called on two experts—historian Dr. John Horner and Dr. F. M. Carter, an expert on contemporary Oregon coastal Indian cultures—to examine the skeletons to see what they might divine. They determined that the larger skeleton was that of a man of African origins, also noting breaks and cracks in his bone that suggested he had suffered significant trauma, and even torture, before he died. The skull from the normal-size skeleton showed an injury consistent with an arrow wound, as well as the type of blunt trauma that would be made by a club. Together, these injuries almost certainly would have been fatal.

This discovery might have been dismissed as interesting, but of no particular importance to the historical record of the Oregon coast—just more proof that over the centuries unnamed men met untimely ends along its wild shore from storms, Indians, or their own companions. But in this case there was more to be contemplated, because for many years it was rumored that pirates had buried a treasure somewhere near the mouth of the Salmon River after their ship had become wrecked in a storm. As their ship lay damaged beyond repair and was pounded to splinters in the booming surf, the buccaneers, as the legend goes, sought a safe place to hide their most prized possession—the loot they had stolen from honest merchant ships on the high seas. So somewhere in the floodplain of the Salmon River they dug a hole, buried a treasure chest, and vanished into the mists of history.

Dr. Carter himself had been told the story of the pirates by his local Indian patients. In their oral tradition, many years ago a ship with great white "wings" had been driven into offshore rocks at the mouth of the Salmon River in a howling gale and slid below the roiling water. About twenty survivors made it to shore, and with them they carried a large chest, which they buried somewhere just a short distance inland. They left two men behind to keep an eye on the treasure, including a very large black man. With their loot secured, the rest of the crew began walking in search of help, although in which direction they headed and what became of them has not been recorded.

The way the Indians told it, the two men eventually got into a vicious argument, although over what isn't certain, and the black man killed the other man. Shortly thereafter, the Indians killed the black man, ostensibly for being a troublemaker. Having no use for or understanding of treasure, the Indians did not look for the buried chest. How the two men came to be buried on top of each other on the beach is not known. Perhaps the Indians buried them so that if their companions returned, they would not know their fate; or perhaps the burial was a result of the natural process of sand blown by the wind or moved by the sea.

The discovery of the two skeletons seems to corroborate the old stories. Moreover, at one time the remains of what could have been an old shipwreck lay sunk just off the coast at that spot, further suggesting that the tale may be true. But so far, the sands at Three Rocks Beach have yet to yield pirate treasure.

As intriguing as the tale of Three Rocks Beach is, Oregon's most famous and oft-told buried-treasure story concerns the gold and silver coins supposedly buried in a chest somewhere on Neahkahnie Mountain and guarded for all eternity by the ghost of a dead man.

At 1,621 feet high and overlooking the Pacific Ocean just north of Nehalem Bay in Tillamook County, Neahkahnie Mountain is a major Oregon coastal landmark. It was long populated by Native Americans, and it was here that they hunted game and picked wild berries. Local Indian tribes incorporated into their oral histories the day when white men arriving from the sea buried a treasure chest on their mountain.

While there are some variations, the basic story told by local Indians to white settlers in the late 1800s relates that one day long ago a sailing ship dropped anchor off the Nehalem Spit and a party of white men rowed ashore in a longboat. Riding the surf onto the beach, they leaped out and dragged the boat onto the sand above the waterline. Next, they hauled out of the boat a chest filled with gold and silver coins and carried it a short distance up the southwest side of Neahkahnie Mountain, where they dug a hole and lowered the chest down. Then one of the men, presumably the leader, drew his flintlock pistol, cocked it, and pulled the trigger. With a roar and a flash of black-powder smoke, one of their number fell to the ground dead. They threw his body in the hole on top of the chest and then shoveled the dirt back in. But before leaving, they dragged a large rock from nearby and, as the Indians watched from hiding, carved some inscriptions into it. Finally, they laid the rock upon the spot where the treasure was interred. Satisfied with their work, the men trekked back down to the beach, rowed out to the waiting ship, and sailed off, confident that the ghost of the dead man would protect the site from interlopers until they were able to return and reclaim their treasure.

A number of slightly different versions of the tale exist. In one version, no one is killed and buried with the chest; in another version, after completing their task, all the pirates, which they are assumed to be, were fallen upon by Indians and massacred.

The legend of the buried treasure of Neahkahnie Mountain is often associated with a tale concerning a Spanish galleon filled with beeswax that shipwrecked just south of the Nehalem Spit probably in the early 1700s. Most believe that these are two separate incidents, in which the Spanish galleon met its end on the Oregon shore, whereas the ship that off-loaded a treasure sailed away unscathed. The fact that the two are sometimes confused suggests they both may have occurred during the same general time frame.

Still another story, derived from Clatsop Indian tales, tells of a damaged Portuguese ship that beached on the coast somewhere around Nehalem Bay, where the crew intended to repair her and sail off. But a violent storm suddenly blew in, destroying the ship and scattering the crew. To escape, the men ran into Neahkahnie Mountain, where they disappeared. Before they departed into the wilds, the Indians observed the crew haul a heavy chest out of the ruined ship and bury it on the beach. Because the crewmen had curly hair, the Indians eventually referred to them as Portuguese as the story was handed down over the decades.

Still another version says that a great sea battle between three ships was fought off the coast and witnessed by local Indians. Between cannonball damage and rough seas, one ship was eventually destroyed, and the survivors hauled a chest to shore and buried it, but not before killing one of their crewman, a black man, and depositing him in the hole with the chest.

A children's version of the story, which early white settlers told their offspring at bedtime, eventually evolved. In this tale, the "queen's royal ship" was on its way home loaded with gold, jewels, and other valuables when it was set upon by a pirate ship off the Oregon coast. In an attempt to escape, the crew landed near Neahkahnie Mountain and buried their valuable cargo to hide it from the pirates. Unfortunately, the pirates captured the crew, and when the queen's loyal sailors refused to betray the treasure's location, all were killed. Parents usually waited until their children were older to tell the rest of the tale so as not to frighten them: According to legend, the sailors' ghosts guard the queen's treasure, and they will haunt to death anyone who finds and takes it.

Unlike the treasure of Three Rocks Beach, the rumored gold and silver buried at Neahkahnie Mountain has launched many an expedition to find it. From the mid-1800s into the 1940s, numerous concerted efforts to search the mountain slopes and beaches for clues were made. However, no map exists, and the only known directions to the treasure, which have been passed down over the years, are not very useful: "Travel one mile east of the beach at Neahkahnie to an enormous fir tree, then travel two hundred yards south to a big rock."

One of the first known treasure hunters was a Tillamook County settler named Hiram Smith. Smith had married an elderly woman of the Clatsop tribe. According to rumor, he wed her specifically to obtain information about the treasure of Neahkahnie Mountain—information that he thought only the spouse of a tribal member might be told. She purportedly told him that the money was buried on the mountain at a fork in a small headwater stream. Unable to identify a location resembling her description, Smith nevertheless found a spot he thought was promising and excavated the area for several years. He finally gave up after discovering, for all his effort, only an old drainpipe.

In 1890 his son Pat, who often tagged along on his father's expeditions, continued the family tradition, eventually locating three or four rocks with pictograph characters scratched into them. Indeed, the legends said that the rocks marking the buried treasure had just such carvings. By 1897 Smith the younger had dug up another rock that he thought was carved with directions to the treasure. He followed his interpretations of the markings to the spot where an old, large, dead spruce tree still stood, believing that another clue to the treasure's location would be found somewhere along its base. But, alas, he came to a dead end and gave up the search in discouragement.

In the following years many men scoured the mountain, shovels in hand, seeking the gold and silver coin of legend. Even Pat Smith returned in 1915 for one more (unsuccessful) try. By now the search for the treasure of Neahkahnie was becoming something of a circus. Three Swedes tried to find the treasure by divining a "magic" spot, while two brothers from Portland built a "treasure compass" with a brass cylinder and wires that would give them the treasure's coordinates. Another treasure hunter was sure he had discovered the chest when his shovel hit something that sounded hollow, only to discover that it was a rock lodged above a rodent tunnel. At one point, two local boys drew a treasure map as a prank and passed it off to a hapless treasure seeker who dutifully followed its arrows and lines into the forest. But treasure hunting on the mountain could be dangerous, and at least one man died in a cave-in while excavating a deep hole.

With all the digging going on, various old items and artifacts were unearthed, and some were interpreted to be associated with the treasure chest. These included a couple of old brass handles that were said to have come from the chest itself, as well as about twenty chunks of oddly shaped pieces of iron tucked in a row against a log in the forest, although no one could provide any plausible connection between these metal bits and the treasure.

One of the largest and most organized efforts to find the treasure of Neahkahnie was launched in 1946 by a group of men who had formed a partnership for that purpose. Charlie Pike, a former companion of Pat Smith's during previous searches, was a member of the team.

Choosing their spot based on information about the treasure gleaned from what they claimed were heretofore-unknown sources, the four partners set to work with a rented bulldozer. But that effort recovered only dirt and debris. So they dragged a gasoline-powered drill onto the mountain and gouged out a forty-foot-deep shaft into the earth. Convinced that success was imminent, they persevered with the zeal of gold prospectors who are certain they are about to become rich if they look just a little longer. But after a year of toil and no treasure, their hopes collapsed along with the partnership. Despite the complete failure of all these searches, many residents of the Nehalem area believe the treasure does exist and still lies buried somewhere on Neahkahnie Mountain.

A question that the treasure hunters seldom ask is why pirates would bury the loot they plundered during their oceanic depredations in some remote location when it makes more sense for them to head for the nearest safe port to spend it on shallow pleasures and frivolous trinkets. But to ponder that question too deeply would spoil the hopes of a buried-treasure hunter. And, in fact, there do seem to be a few cases of pirates who may have buried some of their treasure, including Captain William Kidd and Sir Francis Drake. Treasure maps, however, are a different story. The idea of such a document—crudely scratched on weathered parchment where X marks the spot—in all likelihood originated in such popular fiction as Robert Louis Stevenson's epic buccaneer tale *Treasure Island.*

While decades-long searches for buried pirate treasure at Three Rocks Beach and Neahkahnie Mountain make good stories, and rumors of men killed and buried along with it add spice to the tale, Oregon's most chilling tale of buried treasure is the legend of the Cursed Treasure of Columbia City.

Columbia City was established in 1867 on the Oregon bank of the Columbia River, about seventy-five miles from its mouth. The town's founders hoped it would grow large and wealthy as the northern terminus of the Willamette Valley Railroad, thus making it an important shipping port. But these dreams fell through when the railroad's owner, Benjamin Holladay, lost his fortune in the financial crash of 1873. Today, Columbia City (population: about 1,600) is a bedroom community for the city of St. Helens, a few miles upstream.

But in 1841, twenty-six years before the city was founded, a Spanish bark (a small, three-mast sailing ship) was said to have landed on this site to take on water for its thirsty crew. By the time the first crewman leaped ashore, the grisly legend of a cursed treasure had already been set in motion.

Spain has a long history along the Oregon coast and the Columbia River. Commanding the ship *Santiago,* Captain Bruno de Hezeta—for whom Heceta Head was named—made the first European sighting of the river's mouth in 1775. Sixteen years later, Spanish ships began penetrating the lower river. And when word of Lewis and Clark's successful expedition reached Spain in 1806, the Spanish government was livid that the Americans had entered territory they claimed as theirs. But by the 1840s Spanish power had waned in the Pacific Northwest, including Oregon, as the United States was beginning to establish permanent settlements in the region. Still, trade continued, and ships from many countries, including Spain, plied the coast, rivers, and bays.

Presumably, the vessel that put in along the shore of the Columbia River that day in 1841 was one of those many commercial ships, although its name, business, and destination have not survived in the historical records.

What has been recorded is that the ship was carrying cargo of great value and that the crew was made up of a collection of men whose trust could only be guaranteed by armed officers. To reduce the chance of mutiny, the bark's captain and officers had made great effort to hide the nature of their valuable cargo. But secrets are hard to keep on board a ship at sea. The men came to learn that what was in the hold would make them rich men, and they hatched a murderous plot, which they carried out as soon as the anchor was dropped. By the time the first treacherous sailor set foot ashore, the captain and officers were dead.

Now, with the rich cargo theirs, it was time to distribute the booty. But greed, along with murder, ruled the day, and fights broke out over how to divvy up the loot. Several of the mutineers were killed in the melee. As word spread that a ship had landed along the river, Indians began to arrive. Between the sudden violence that erupted among the sailors and the presence of a large number of Indians, the remaining sailors became nervous and decided to bury the valuables for safekeeping. After finishing the job, they retreated to the ship and waited for the Indians to depart. But much to their dismay, the natives pitched their lodges along the shoreline and made all appearances of planning to stay. Deeming it too risky to put ashore again and retrieve the loot, the crew sailed off, vowing to return later and claim their treasure.

After two years of wandering the sea, the crew returned to the site and once again put ashore. Led by the man who had directed the burial of the loot, the sailors trekked to the spot where it lay, but to their shock they could not find it— the ground appeared as if nothing had ever been buried there. Shaken and confused, the men went back to their ship, only to discover that the man who led them to the treasure site had vanished, and they could not find him anywhere. Doubly alarmed, the crew boarded their ship, sailed downriver to the Pacific Ocean, and never came back.

Over the years, stories of the buried treasure, believed to be in the form of gold coins, were passed around in the small towns and settlements that had sprung up along the Columbia River waterfront. Forty years after the theft of the bark's cargo and the murder of its officers, a group of treasure seekers made an attempt to find the buried lucre—an endeavor the survivors would live to regret.

Sometime in the year 1881, a group of spiritualists gathered in Columbia City for a conclave (the late nineteenth century was a time when interest in the occult was on the rise, especially among the upper classes). One of the mediums claimed that she had received information from the spirit world pinpointing the exact place where the crew of the Spanish bark had buried their loot.

A group of them ventured out, guided by the medium and her spirit helper, to the supposed treasure site. They began to dig furiously, soon unearthing piles of broken rocks not more than a foot or so below the surface. But they had barely begun to toss the rocks aside in anxious anticipation of what lay beneath when one of the spiritualists staggered, rolled his eyes, and collapsed dead onto the freshly turned-up dirt. The medium, in a trance, announced that the ghost of the bark's long-dead captain, who remained there to guard the cargo his employers had entrusted him with, had killed their companion. The cargo had been stolen from him once, but he would not let it be stolen a second time. Horrified, the surviving members of the party fled back to

Columbia City. News of the terrible event so unnerved all who heard the story that no one wanted to even think about the treasure of Columbia City anymore, much less search for it.

For nearly a decade, fear kept the buried treasure safe from interlopers. Then, in March 1890, another group of treasure seekers set out to find it for themselves, although whether they were aware of the fate of the last party of searchers is not known.

They managed to locate the site the first group had discovered with the assistance of supernatural forces. They began digging, encountering the same layer of broken stones their predecessors had. Tossing the rocks aside, they continued digging through layers of soil until they made a chilling discovery—four or five human skeletons, almost surely those of the mutinous Spanish sailors who died in the long-ago quarrel over how their stolen booty should be divided. The digging party examined the skeletons more closely, perhaps thinking they might contain more clues to the treasure's whereabouts, or perhaps just out of morbid curiosity. As they contemplated bits of rib cage and grinning skulls, one of the party began to shake uncontrollably, his eyes bugging out. Then the man fell to the ground, twitching and screaming, going mad before the others' eyes. That was enough for this crew of treasure hunters, and they scattered in panic, never to return.

To this day no one else has returned either, partly because the location of the treasure site has been lost. The stories say it was buried on what eventually became Hez Copler's farm, but there

are no historical records of a farmer by that name owning property in the area. But some will tell you that the real reason is fear
of the ghostly guardian of the Cursed Treasure of Columbia City,
and what he does to those who would try to steal what is his.

True or not, the Cursed Treasure of Columbia City may be
a cautionary tale for all would-be buried-treasure seekers. Tales
of buried treasure, in Oregon at least, are tales of gold, silver,
and other valuables of suspect origin, buried by men of dubious
character who, before they sail away, often leave a body or two
behind. Buried treasure may be less adventure and riches than
larceny and murder, all coiled together in a dark hole. Before
putting spade to earth, contemporary treasure hunters would do
well to consider what they may really be digging up.

BIBLIOGRAPHY

Adams, Cecil. "Did Pirates Bury Their Treasure?" www.straight dope.com.

Associated Press. "Some of the Ransom Money from D. B. Cooper Hijacking Is to Be Auctioned." *The Dallas Morning News,* April 1, 2008.

———. "Did Children Find D. B. Cooper's Parachute?" www .msnbc.msn.com, March 26, 2008.

———. "Did D. B. Cooper Retire to Oregon Coast?" KATU .com, July 27, 2008.

———. "FBI Makes New Bid to Find 1971 Skyjacker." *San Francisco Chronicle,* January 2, 2008.

———. "FBI Rejects Latest D. B. Cooper Suspect." *Seattle Post-Intelligencer,* October 26, 2007.

———. "A Gateway to Controversy." KGW.com, October 7, 2007.

———. "Parachute 'Absolutely Not D. B. Cooper's.'" www .msnbc.msn.com, April 1, 2008.

Atwater, Brian, Musumi-Rokkaku Satoko, Satake Kenji, Tsuji Yoshinobu, Ueda Kazue, and David K. Yamaguchi. "The Orphan Tsunami of 1700." U.S. Geological Survey. Seattle: University of Washington Press, 2005.

Baker, Mark. "Shadowing Bigfoot." *The Register-Guard* (Eugene, Ore.), December 17, 2006.

Barnard, Jeff. "Mysterious Oregon Vortex Is a Swirl of Controversy." *The Seattle Times,* April 1, 2004.

Bigfoot Field Research Organization, www.bfro.net.

Bigfoot History, www.bigfoot-lives.com.

Bigfoot Museums, www.chat111.com/Bigfoot_Museums.

Borgard, Doug. "Port Orford Redux: John Evans, Scientist or Charlatan?" *Meteorite Magazine* 13, no. 2 (May 2007): 24–27.

———. "Port Orford Redux, Part II: Discovery or Deception?" *Meteorite Magazine* 13, no. 3 (May 2007): 9–12.

Caims, Peter. "Colossal Claude and the Sea Monsters." *Oregonian* (Portland), September 24, 1967.

Campbell, Louis. Siuslaw Pioneer Museum, Florence, Ore. Personal communication.

Carkhuff, David. "Bigfoot Feat: Remarkable Hoax Looms Large in Grant County Family's History." *Blue Mountain Eagle* (John Day, Ore.), December 25, 2002.

"Codename: Norjak. The Skyjacking of Northwest Flight 305." http://Check-Six.com.

Cook, Warren L. *Flood Tide of History.* New Haven: Yale University Press, 1973.

Coreno, Catherine. "D. B. Cooper Timeline." *New York Magazine,* October 22, 2007.

D. B. Cooper, Portrait of an American Hijacker. Filiquarian Publishing, 2008.

"D. B. Cooper Redux." Federal Bureau of Investigation, Headline Archives, December 7, 2007.

D. B. Cooper. Vancouver, Wash.: The Columbian, 1989.

Daegling, David J. *Bigfoot Exposed.* Walnut Creek, Calif.: Alta Mira Press, 2004.

Deur, Douglas. "A Most Sacred Place." *Oregon Historical Quarterly,* Spring 2002, 18–49.

DeVoto, Bernard. *The Course of Empire.* Boston: Houghton Mifflin, 1952.

Dillon, H. Richard. *Shanghaiing Days.* New York: Coward-McCann, 1961.

Dixon, Schuyler. "Man Who Finds Money Linked to D. B. Cooper Skyjacking to Auction Off Cash." *Oregonian* (Portland), March 31, 2008.

Duewel, Jeff. "Encounter at the Caves." *Daily Courier* (Grants Pass, Ore.), August 5, 2006.

Elliot, T. C. "Journal of David Thompson." *Oregon Historical Society Quarterly,* March–June 1914.

Evans, John W. "Powerful Rocky: The Blue Mountains and the Oregon Trail, 1811–1883." La Grande, Ore.: Pika Press, Eastern Oregon State College, 1991.

Everhart, Mike. "Pliosaurid or Polycotylid." www.oceansof kansas.com/pliosaur.html.

Finucane, Stephanie. "Heceta House: A History and Architectural Survey." Forest Service–USDA. *Studies in Cultural Resource Management* 3 (1985).

Fleagle, Judy. "Haunted Structures and Ghostly Happenings." *Oregon Coast Magazine* (September–October 2008): 50–55.

Frazier, Joseph B. "Waterfront: Sea Captains in Need of Crews in Portland Could Buy a Drugged Would-Be Sailor for a Few Dollars." *The Press-Enterprise* (Riverside, Calif.), May 19, 2001.

Gibbs, James A., Jr. *Sentinels of the North Pacific.* Portland: Binfords & Mort, Publishers, 1955.

Gibbs, Philip. "I Know a Place Where Things Seem to Roll Uphill. How Does It Work?" Division of Physical and Mathematical Sciences, University of California–Riverside, 1996.

Giesecke, E. W. "Beeswax and Castaways: Searching for Oregon's Protohistoric Asian Ship." Paper presented at the 47th Annual Meeting of the Society for the History of Discoveries, Portland, Oregon, September 7–9, 2006.

Gilden, Jennifer D. "Environment, Symbolism and Changing Gender Roles in Oregon's Santiam Canyon." Master's thesis, Oregon State University, December 4, 1996.

Gilmore, Susan. "D. B. Cooper Puzzle: The Legend Turns 30." *Seattle Times,* November 22, 2001.

Grant, John, and Ray Jones. *Legendary Lighthouses.* Old Saybrook, Conn.: Globe Pequot Press, 1998.

Helm, Mike. *Oregon's Ghosts and Monsters.* Eugene, Ore.: Rainy Day Press, 1983.

Henderson, E. P., and Hollis M. Dole. "The Port Orford Meteorite." *The Ore Bin* 26, no. 7 (July 1964): 113–130.

Hill, Richard. "Hunting for the Past, Beeswax Ship Researchers Want to Separate the Legend from the Truth." *Oregonian* (Portland), May 23, 2006.

———. "Landslide Sleuths." *Oregonian* (Portland), May 15, 2002.

———. "A New Look at an Old Landslide." *Oregonian* (Portland), September 29, 1999.

Hoffman, Charles S. *The Search for Oregon's Lost Blue Bucket Mine.* Medford, Ore.: Webb Research Group, 1992.

Holland, F. Ross. *Lighthouses.* New York: Metro Books, 1995.

Hult, Ruby E. *Lost Mines and Treasures of the Pacific Northwest.* Portland: Binfords & Mort, 1957.

"Investigator Claims He Found D. B. Cooper—in Oregon."
KGW.com, May 30, 2008.

Johnson, Daniel M., Richard R. Petersen, D. Richard Lycan,
James M. Sweet, and Mark E. Neuhaus. *Atlas of Oregon
Lakes.* Corvallis: Oregon State University Press, 1985.

Jones, Suzi, and Jarold Ramsey. "The Stories We Tell."
Corvallis: Oregon State University Press, 1994.

Jung, Helen. "Portland's Buried Truth." *Oregonian* (Portland),
October 4, 2007.

Kershaw, Sarah. "Tourist Draw for Sale, with Mystery the
Lure." *New York Times,* November 28, 2008.

Kettler, Bill. "Collings Mountain Trail Offers Look at Bigfoot
Trap." *Mail Tribune* (Medford, Ore.), May 4, 2007.

"Lady of the Lighthouse Baffles Workmen." *Siuslaw News*
(Reedsport, Ore.), November 26, 1975.

"A Lake of Mystery." *New York Times,* April 27, 1902.

Lansing, Jewel. *Portland, People, Politics, and Power,
1851–2001.* Corvallis: Oregon State University Press, 2005.

Lawrence, Donald B. "The Submerged Forest of the Columbia
River Gorge." *Geographical Review* 26, no. 4 (October 1936):
581–592.

Leffingwell, Randy, and Pamela Welty. *Lighthouses of the Pacific
Coast.* Stillwater, Minn.: Voyageur Press, 2000.

Litster, John. "The Oregon Vortex, Notes and Data." The Oregon Vortex, Gold Hill, 1960.

Lockwood, Brad. "The Devil of the Deschutes." *The Source Weekly* (Bend, Ore.), December 13, 2007.

McArthur, Lewis A. *Oregon Geographic Names.* Portland: Oregon Historical Society Press, 1982.

McNerthney, Casey. "D. B. Cooper, Where Are You?" *Seattle Post-Intelligencer,* November 23, 2007.

Meldrum, Jeff. "Sasquatch: Legend Meets Science." *Talk of the Nation,* National Public Radio, November 10, 2006.

Mendelson, Aaron. "Shanghai Tunnels!" *The Quest* (Reed College, Portland), September 24, 2008.

"A Metropolis Rises on Sacks of Grain, Cans of Salmon and the Backs of Indentured Servants." www.portlandwaterfront.org/1870_1899.html.

Morrell, Virginia. "Sea Monsters." *National Geographic Magazine,* December 2005.

Mortenson, Eric. "Ghost Inhabits Coast Home." *The Bend Bulletin,* January 1, 1995.

Mysterious Creatures. Alexandria, Va.: Time-Life Books, 1988.

O'Conner, Jim E. "The Evolving Landscape of the Columbia River Gorge, Lewis and Clark and Cataclysms on the Columbia." *Oregon Historical Quarterly* 1, no. 3 (Fall 2004).

Oregon Bigfoot Sightings Database, www.oregonbigfoot.com.

Pinyerd, David. *Lighthouses and Life-Saving on the Oregon Coast.* San Francisco: Arcadia Publishing, 2007.

Plotkin, Howard. *The Port Orford Oregon Meteorite Hoax.* Smithsonian Contributions to the Earth Sciences, No. 3. Washington, D.C.: Smithsonian Institution Press, 1993.

"Ports of the World: Portland, Oregon, USA." The Maritime Heritage Project, www.maritimeheritage.org/ports/usOregon Portland.html.

Ramsayer, Kate. "Seeking Sasquatch, a Group of Enthusiasts Come Here to Track the Elusive Mythical Beast." *Bend Bulletin,* June 24, 2007.

Rebuffoni, Dean. "Hijacker's Note at First Mistaken as Date Invitation." *Star Tribune* (Minneapolis–St. Paul), November 27, 1971.

"A Sea Cow, the Monster Seen in Wallowa Lake by a Prospector." *Wallowa County Chieftain* (Joseph, Ore.), November 5, 1885.

The Search for Bigfoot, www.oregonlive.com/special/current/bigfoot.ssf.

Skolnik, Sam. "30 Years Ago, D. B. Cooper's Night Leap Began a Legend." *Seattle Post-Intelligencer,* November 22, 2001.

Smitten, Susan. *Ghost Stories of Oregon*. Auburn, Wash.: Lone Pine Publishing International, 2001.

Swart, Rick. "Atomic Ducks Dive for 'Treasure' at Wallowa Lake." *Wallowa County Chieftain* (Joseph, Ore.), December 15, 2008.

Tedford, Deborah. "FBI Seeks Help in Solving Skyjacking Mystery." www.npr.org, January 2, 2008.

"TV Crew to Film Lighthouse Ghost Today." *Siuslaw News* (Reedsport, Ore.), September 20, 2000.

"25 Years Ago." *Siuslaw News* (Reedsport, Ore.), November 29, 2000.

"Two Indian Legends." Whitman Mission National Historic Site archives, National Park Service.

United Press International. "D. B. Cooper Money Split." *New York Times,* May 23, 1986.

Unser, Mike. "D. B. Cooper Notes Make $37K at Heritage's Americana Memorabilia Auction." www.coinnews.net, June 13, 2008.

"U.S. Lawyer Believes Notorious Fugitive D. B. Cooper Hid Ransom Money in Vcr Bank." *Canadian Press* (Vancouver, B.C.), August 4, 2008.

Walsh, Edward. "D. B. Cooper's Chute Found?" *Oregonian* (Portland), March 26, 2008.

———. "Mystery Lives On, Even If D. B. Doesn't." *Oregonian* (Portland), November 25, 2007.

Weaver, Russ. "Use of Dendrochronology to Date and Better Understand the Bonneville Landslide, Columbia River Gorge, Washington." *Geological Society of America Abstracts with Programs* 35, no. 6 (September 2003): 80.

Williams, Chuck. *Bridge of the Gods, Mountains of Fire.* San Francisco: Friends of the Earth and Elephant Mountain Arts, 1980.

Williams, Scott S. "A Research Design to Conduct Archaeological Investigations at the Site of the Beeswax Wreck of Nehalem Bay, Tillamook County, Oregon." Beeswax Shipwreck Project, Olympia, Wash., December 2006.

Worcester, Thomas K. *Bunco Kelly and Other Yarns of Portland and Northwest Oregon.* Beaverton, Ore.: TMS Book Service, 1983.

www.museum.bmi.net. *Beeswax Wreck 2007 Newsletter,* Beeswax Shipwreck Project, Olympia, Wash., June 15, 2007.

INDEX

A

America
    construction of
      lighthouses in, 70–72
    lake monsters in, 114–15
    shanghaiing in, 130,
      131–32
    vortex sites in, 107
    westward migration in,
      57–59
Anderson, Harold E., 3, 5
Anderson, Jim, 76–77
Astoria, shanghaiing in,
    140–41

B

beeswax, 87–88, 94, 95
    at Nehalem beach, 83, 84,
      95–97
Beeswax Shipwreck Project, 98
Betts, J. P., 136
Bigfoot, 15–28
    Chetco River encounter,
      20–22
    Deschutes County
      sightings, 19, 26–27
    organizations studying,
      24–26

    Wallace's hoaxes, 27–28
Bigfoot Field Researchers
    Organization, 25
Blue Bucket Mine. *See* Lost
    Blue Bucket Mine
Boggs, Nancy, 142–43
Bonneville Landslide. *See*
    Columbia River Gorge
Boston Society of Natural
    History, 46, 48, 56
Bridge of the Gods. *See also*
    Columbia River Gorge, 30,
    31, 36, 40, 42
    Native American story of,
      31–33
Bridge of Tomaniwuas. *See*
    Bridge of the Gods
Bunch, George W., 66
Bushnell, David, 49

C

Calkins, E. G., 147, 148, 150
Carter, F. M.,
    150, 151
Cascade Rapids. *See also*
    Columbia River Gorge, 30,
    31, 33
Cascadia earthquake, 41

ABOUT THE AUTHOR

Jim Yuskavitch has been a freelance writer since 1993. In addition to publishing numerous magazine articles, he is the author of *Oregon Wildlife Viewing Guide*, *52 Oregon Nature Weekends*, *Fishing Oregon*, and *Outlaw Tales of Oregon* and co-author of the *Insiders' Guide to Bend and Central Oregon*. He lives in Sisters, Oregon, with his wife, Nikki.